11/07/98

The
International
Pictograms
Standard

Written and Developed by Todd Pierce,
Design Pacifica International, LLC

Published by ST Publications, Inc.
Cincinnati, Ohio

publications inc.

For more information contact:
ST Publications Book Division
407 Gilbert Avenue
Cincinnati, Ohio 45202
U.S.A.

Book design:
Copyright © 1996 Design Pacifica
International, LLC
Credits: *Text edited by Beverly Bailey;
Graphic design: Todd Pierce, Jason West*

Printed in the United States of America
Riddle Press   1-800-536-5751
4555 SW Main Avenue
Beaverton, OR 97005

ISBN: 0-944094-22-8

Contents

Introduction

This book is about international pictograms. Many words will describe a pictogram - ideogram, icon, symbol sign, pictograph, pictorial symbol, etc. I use them all interchangeably in the pages that follow. But "pictogram" is my favorite. It says all that needs to be said. "Icon," on the other hand, conveys deity-like overtones. " Pictograph" can mean a chart or graph. And "symbol" has several meanings. "Pictogram" simply sums up the reality it defines: "picto," meaning "picture" and "-gram," conveying "message," as in *telegram*. But make no mistake, this is not a book about words. It is about something more basic: communication, a means of communication that can be simplified and understood by everyone. It is about a quest to improve communication within today's global metropolis, bridging language barriers and simplifying basic messages.

And more. This book is also about a study that took place over the course of one year in Portland, Oregon. It is about the goals of that study, the process developed, and the results it produced. We had one grand concept - to create a perpetual study. And one primary goal - to introduce an International Pictograms Standard throughout the world. We looked to the world for help in creating this standard. We look in the same direction to keep it fresh and "alive."

You will find a scoring sheet inside. I hope you will use it. Fill it out and mail it to me. Your input is not only welcome; it is imperative. For a standard to reach worldwide status, it must have more than one author. The International Pictograms Standard is for everyone to share, implement and improve.

I look forward to your input! Enjoy the book.

Todd Pierce
President
Design Pacifica International, LLC

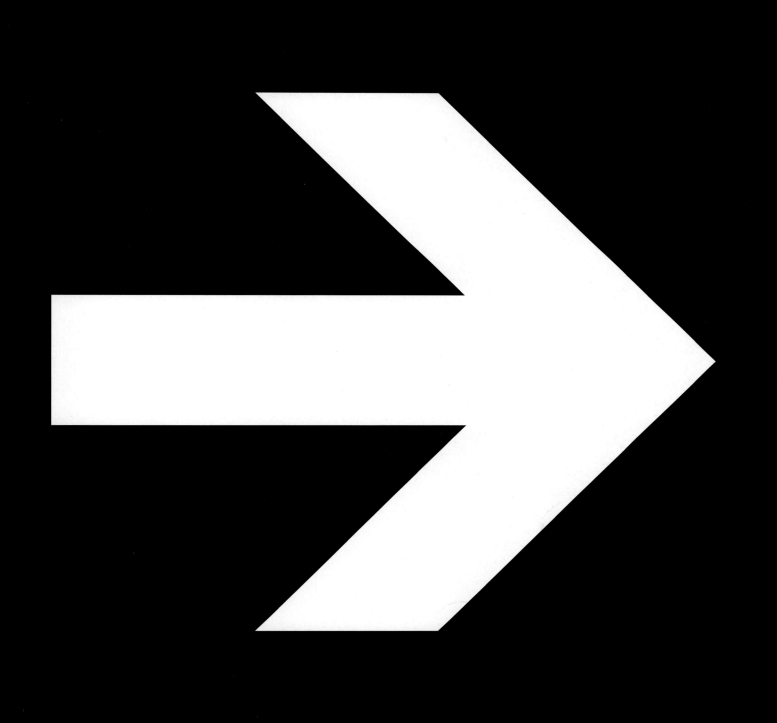

History of Pictograms
Chapter 1

Early forms of communication

We can trace humankind's use of pictorial symbols, or pictograms as they are often called today, to abstract prehistoric markings inscribed on rocks and the walls of caves. By 2,000 B.C., the Egyptians had created simplified images that eventually led to the replacement of symbolic pictures with phonetic writing. Over the centuries, languages evolved, adding enormous variety to the communication process. With over one hundred languages and six thousand dialects in the world today, international communication has become overwhelmingly complex.

Over the past three hundred years, several attempts have been made to create a universal method of communication by returning to the simple picture symbols used by early man. Innovations such as the International System of Typographic Picture Education symbols (ISOTYPE) created by Otto Neurath in the 1920s and the Semantography symbols designed by Charles Bliss in the 1940s have inspired a widespread belief that symbolism is the best and most effective tool for giving and receiving information internationally.

1974 AIGA / D.O.T. Symbol Signs study

By the 1970s, twenty-eight different sets of pictograms were in use throughout the world. However, none of these sets comprised a complete standard that was both graphically consistent and appropriate for international recognition. In 1974, the American Institute of Graphic Arts (AIGA), commissioned by the U.S. Department of Transportation (D.O.T.), and supported by a National Endowment for the Arts grant, established a committee to develop a single uniform and internationally recognized symbol set. The AIGA committee, headed by Thomas H. Geismar, developed criteria for evaluating existing pictogram sets. The goal was to establish a consistent and interrelated collection of symbols to bridge language barriers and simplify basic messages for transportation facilities around the world. Through widespread promotion, acceptance and use, this standard set of signs has become the most commonly used set of pictograms in the world.

Pictograms for a "global" metropolis

Still, the D.O.T. Symbol Signs set of pictograms, which addresses primarily transportation-related messages, serves a limited purpose. Over the past twenty years, organizations throughout the world have labored to create additional standard sets.

Three are especially noteworthy. In 1985, the Army Corps of Engineers, under the design direction of Don Meeker, developed a set of National Recreation Symbols for use by the National Park Service. In 1994, a University of Cincinnati student, Brendan Murphy, supported by a grant from the

Society for Environmental Graphic Design (SEGD), created some exciting improvements to icons used by the disabled. Most recently, the Atlanta Committee for the Olympic Games selected a five-member design team to develop a comprehensive graphics program, including a new set of pictograms, for use at the 1996 Summer Olympic Games.

Every successful new set of pictorial symbols, however helpful, serves only one area of human endeavor. What about a universal set of pictograms covering the full range of public activities? Would it be possible to design a study for the purpose of developing an internationally recognized, universal standard set?

In August 1994, the Portland, Oregon Visitors Association (POVA) called on my firm, Design Pacifica International, to help the city of Portland better serve its rapidly-expanding ranks of foreign visitors. It had become painfully obvious that no single set of pictograms in existence would cope with the needs of today's "global" metropolis. How could we create standard, internationally recognized pictorial symbols to convey messages about every area of urban life? We would have to find common pictograms for transportation, public services, direction and egress, hotel and lodging, outdoors and sports activities, rules and regulations and the needs of

the disabled (in compliance with the Americans with Disabilities Act). Could this be accomplished?

Example of Brendan Murphy's mobility symbol designs.

The Portland Project

Chapter 2

A Standard for the City

In August 1994, the Portland Oregon Visitors Association (POVA) International Subcommittee recommended that a standard set of pictograms be adopted for use by both public and private organizations in the Portland metropolitan area. The group believed that the widespread use of consistent and effective pictograms would further Portland's continuing campaign to attract and maintain international tourism, trade, and investment.

Later that month, Dwight Trahin, facilities manager of Portland's World Trade Center and a member of the International Subcommittee, contacted me. At the time, my firm was completing the design of an exterior sign program for World Trade Center Portland. Because of the large contingent of international visitors that frequented the facility, we had, coincidently, begun considering pictograms to convey messages on our signs. Dwight suggested that I present a brief review of our work, as well as a look at the history and current uses of pictograms, at a meeting of his subcommittee.

The presentation took place later that month. Because no single set of pictograms existed to convey the multitude of messages required for an entire city, committee members believed a comprehensive set would have to be created. It was my opinion that designing a new set would be unwise, since so many common symbols were already employed around the world. The committee agreed, and proposed to begin the monumental task of collecting available pictograms and symbol sets from around the world.

It soon became apparent that a work plan was necessary to properly approach the development of a city-wide pictograms standard. We needed to create a process. First, we would have to gather pictograms from around the world and categorize them by message. Then, we would need to evaluate them and select the best for inclusion in our new standard. Most importantly, the new standard would have to be officially adopted by every bureau and agency within the city and aggressively promoted within the private sector to encourage its acceptance and future use.

The evaluation process

Over the next six months, we collected several hundred individual pictograms and many symbol sets. Existing sets included the D.O.T. Symbol Signs, the Army Corps of Engineers' National Recreation symbols, SEGD's ADA Symbols of Accessibility, and pictogram sets from the American Hotel & Motel Association and the Oregon Lodging Association, among others. All were assembled into a review and selection workbook. Next, we created categories based on user needs within an urban environment.

The subcommittee, which was headed by Andrew Haruyama, director of international relations for the Mayor's Office, then distributed the workbooks to over sixty city bureaus, agencies and organizations. At a series of review meetings, our overall goals were discussed and procedures carefully laid down.

We decided to employ a scoring process similar to that used in the 1974 AIGA / D.O.T. Symbol Signs study. Evaluation criteria were designed to allow committee members and others participating in scoring to "grade" the pictograms in three distinct yet interrelated dimensions. They are the same three dimensions present in all visual communication: *semantic*, *syntactic*, and *pragmatic*.

Pictograms were represented individually in the workbooks. We asked participants to circle their responses on a scale of 1 - 5 for each of the three design dimensions, "1" representing the least degree of effectiveness and "5" representing the highest degree of effectiveness. Participants were given the following definitions:

The *semantic dimension* refers to the relationship of a visual image to a meaning.

- *How well does this pictogram represent the message?*
- *Will people understand the message that the pictogram denotes?*
- *Will people from various cultures understand this pictogram?*
- *Will people of various ages understand this pictogram?*
- *Is it easy to learn this pictogram?*
- *Has this pictogram previously been widely accepted?*
- *Does this pictogram contain elements that are unrelated to the message?*

The *syntactic dimension* refers to the relationship of one visual image to another.

- *How well does this pictogram, as a whole, relate to other pictograms?*
- *How well do the elements of this pictogram relate to the elements of other pictograms?*
- *Is the design of this pictogram consistent in its use of figure/ground, solid/outline, overlapping, orientation, format, scale, texture, with other pictograms?*
- *Are the most important elements recognized first?*
- *Does this pictogram seriously contradict existing standards or conventions?*

The *pragmatic dimension* refers to the relationship of a visual image to a user.

- *Can a person see the pictogram?*
- *Is this pictogram seriously affected by poor lighting conditions, oblique viewing angles, and other visual 'noise'?*
- *Does this pictogram remain visible throughout the range of typical viewing distances?*
- *Is this pictogram especially vulnerable to defacing?*

It was important that the final standard include neither too few nor too many pictograms. We wanted to adopt visual images for the kinds of orientation and wayfinding messages most commonly needed. However, we also wanted to avoid visual overload, which would only detract from the public's ability to both see and comprehend vital messages. All participants were therefore asked to mark each pictogram/message in their workbooks to indicate whether or not it should be included in the final standard.

During the two-month period allocated for review and scoring, we were busy developing a software program to enable us to input and automatically tally the results. The program calculated an average score and converted this information into an overall rating percentile for each of the three design dimensions. A rating percentile was also formulated based on the group's indication of whether or not the given pictogram/message should be included or excluded from the standard.

Study results

At the conclusion of the review and selection process, the POVA International Subcommittee met to review the tabulated results. There was a clear disparity between pictograms that rated an overall high score for effectiveness and those that faired poorly. We decided to consider only those pictograms scoring above the fifty percentile for inclusion in the standard. *(Although it can be said that a picture is worth a thousand words, no one wanted a thousand pictograms for every message!)*

Finally, it came time to take a close look at each of the selected pictograms and factors that would strengthen them both individually and as a collection. Digitally-produced illustrations were created for each pictogram selected. Our primary concern was to achieve a cohesive set. Pictogram elements, such as arrows, human figures, flames, etc., were illustrated with consistency and in exact scale with one another. It was determined that a dark field or background with white elements provided an optimal level of legibility (except for those pictograms to be displayed in color). Since our ongoing goal was to avoid designing new pictograms, we limited ourselves to making only necessary alterations.

The following pages display illustrations of the final set of pictograms selected by participants. The collective scoring averages and overall rating percentile are shown next to each pictogram.

	Average Semantic Score	Average Syntactic Score	Average Pragmatic Score	To include in Standard

Transportation

Icon	Name	Average Semantic Score	Average Syntactic Score	Average Pragmatic Score	To include in Standard
	Agriculture	2.7	2.8	2.8	55%
	Air Transportation	4.3	4.5	4.4	88%
	Arriving Flights	2.6	2.9	3.1	67%
	Baggage Check-in	4.2	4.3	4.2	80%
	Baggage Lockers	4.2	3.9	4.0	76%
	Bus	4.7	4.6	4.6	95%
	Car Rental	3.3	3.2	3.4	70%
	Customs	4.2	4.3	4.2	86%
	Departing Flights	3.7	3.7	3.8	70%
	Flight Information	3.7	3.3	3.7	65%
	Gas Station	4.4	4.2	4.3	100%
	Ground Transportation	4.4	4.4	4.2	89%
	Heliport	4.4	4.6	4.6	85%

	Average Semantic Score	Average Syntactic Score	Average Pragmatic Score	To include in Standard
Immigration	3.3	3.8	3.7	67%
Moving Walkway	3.4	3.3	3.2	63%
Rail Transportation	4.2	4.2	4.2	100%
Taxi	4.0	4.1	4.0	71%
Ticket Purchase	3.5	3.6	3.2	56%
Tools	4.0	3.7	3.6	67%
Truck	4.5	4.2	4.1	78%

	Average Semantic Score	Average Syntactic Score	Average Pragmatic Score	To include in Standard
Tunnel	3.9	4.1	3.7	72%
Water Transportation	4.3	3.9	3.8	76%

Services

	Average Semantic Score	Average Syntactic Score	Average Pragmatic Score	To include in Standard
ATM	4.0	3.9	3.8	76%
Bar	4.2	4.2	4.2	90%
Barber Shop/Salon	4.0	4.1	4.0	83%
Cashier	2.9	3.0	2.7	60%

7

	Average Semantic Score	Average Syntactic Score	Average Pragmatic Score	To include in Standard			Average Semantic Score	Average Syntactic Score	Average Pragmatic Score	To include in Standard
Changing Room	4.0	3.9	3.9	80%		Fax Machine	2.8	2.9	3.0	85%
Coffee Shop	4.4	4.3	4.3	95%		Florist	3.2	3.0	3.4	65%
Crosswalk	3.9	3.8	4.1	68%		Ice Cream	4.5	4.1	4.5	77%
Currency Exchange	3.0	3.1	3.1	55%		Information	4.3	4.3	4.2	91%
Dancing	4.0	3.8	3.8	67%		Laundry	3.3	3.0	3.3	65%
Drinking Fountain	4.1	4.0	4.2	85%		Leashed Pets	3.6	3.9	4.0	76%
Falling Rocks	2.3	1.8	2.3	61%		Litter Disposal	4.1	4.1	4.1	72%

	Average Semantic Score	Average Syntactic Score	Average Pragmatic Score	To include in Standard		Average Semantic Score	Average Syntactic Score	Average Pragmatic Score	To include in Standard
Lost & Found	3.4	3.4	3.4	76%	Public Health	3.5	3.3	3.5	57%
Mail	3.7	3.8	3.8	81%	Restaurant	4.1	4.5	4.1	95%
Movie Theater	4.0	3.9	3.8	74%	Shoe Shine	4.2	4.0	3.9	84%
Nursery	3.3	3.6	3.5	60%	Shops	3.0	3.1	2.7	60%
Parking	4.3	4.0	3.8	83%	Smoking	4.5	4.4	4.4	95%
Pharmacy	3.7	3.3	3.3	67%	Snacks	4.0	4.2	4.0	84%
Playroom	3.5	3.2	3.4	58%	Stroller	4.0	3.8	3.9	85%

	Average Semantic Score	Average Syntactic Score	Average Pragmatic Score	To include in Standard
Telephone	4.6	4.5	4.4	86%
Theater/Performing Arts	4.0	3.7	4.0	70%
Toilets (Men)	4.7	4.7	4.3	86%
Toilets (Unisex)	4.4	4.5	4.3	90%
Toilets (Women)	4.8	4.8	4.5	86%
TV/Waiting Room	3.9	3.6	3.6	60%

Direction

	Average Semantic Score	Average Syntactic Score	Average Pragmatic Score	To include in Standard
Arrow (Down & Left)	4.5	4.5	4.3	87%
Arrow (Down & Right)	4.6	4.6	4.4	87%
Arrow (Down)	4.6	4.8	4.9	88%
Arrow (Left)	4.9	4.9	4.9	88%
Arrow (Right)	4.9	4.9	4.9	88%
Arrow (Up & Left)	4.5	4.5	4.6	88%

	Average Semantic Score	Average Syntactic Score	Average Pragmatic Score	To include in Standard
Arrow (Up & Right)	4.5	4.5	4.6	88%
Arrow (Up)	4.9	4.9	4.9	88%
Elevator	4.3	4.4	4.0	82%
Entry	2.1	2.4	2.6	53%
Escalator	3.8	4.0	3.8	64%
Escalator (Down)	4.0	4.1	4.0	87%
Escalator (Up)	3.9	4.1	4.0	87%

	Average Semantic Score	Average Syntactic Score	Average Pragmatic Score	To include in Standard
No Entry	2.5	2.5	2.8	71%
Stairs	4.1	4.2	4.2	87%
Stairs (Down)	4.1	4.2	4.2	85%
Stairs (Up)	4.1	4.2	4.2	86%

Lodging

	Average Semantic Score	Average Syntactic Score	Average Pragmatic Score	To include in Standard
Bedroom	4.0	4.1	3.6	76%
Bellman	4.3	3.8	4.0	90%

	Average Semantic Score	Average Syntactic Score	Average Pragmatic Score	To include in Standard
Check-in Registration	4.0	3.8	3.9	65%
Conference Room	4.0	4.0	3.7	71%
Drinking Water	3.3	3.2	3.4	63%
Electrical Outlet	4.1	4.0	3.7	78%
Hotel	3.5	3.7	3.6	60%
Hotel Information	3.5	3.3	3.5	62%
Housekeeping	3.8	3.7	3.8	60%
Ice	3.8	3.3	3.6	85%
Keys	4.5	4.2	4.4	74%
Light Switch	3.3	3.1	3.2	59%
Quiet	3.9	3.5	3.6	65%
Room Key Return	3.5	3.2	3.5	63%
Room Service	4.0	3.8	3.9	75%
Shower	4.5	4.3	4.5	80%

	Average Semantic Score	Average Syntactic Score	Average Pragmatic Score	To include in Standard
Thermostat	3.6	3.6	3.7	79%
Used Razor Blades	4.0	3.7	4.0	81%
Vending Machine	3.7	3.6	3.4	70%

Activities

	Average Semantic Score	Average Syntactic Score	Average Pragmatic Score	To include in Standard
Baseball	4.2	4.3	4.1	65%
Bicycle	4.3	4.4	4.3	76%
Boat Launch	4.3	4.4	4.2	82%

	Average Semantic Score	Average Syntactic Score	Average Pragmatic Score	To include in Standard
Canoeing	4.4	4.4	4.3	78%
Cross-Country Skiing	3.8	3.6	3.8	63%
Deer	3.9	4.1	3.9	62%
Diving	3.5	3.4	3.3	63%
Exercising	3.5	3.4	3.3	63%
Fishing	4.1	3.9	3.6	81%
Golf	4.3	4.3	3.9	87%

	Average Semantic Score	Average Syntactic Score	Average Pragmatic Score	To include in Standard		Average Semantic Score	Average Syntactic Score	Average Pragmatic Score	To include in Standard
Gymnasium	3.8	3.7	3.7	59%	Marina	3.6	3.7	3.9	75%
Hiking Trail	3.8	3.8	3.9	71%	Motor Boating	4.2	4.0	4.1	82%
Horseback Riding	4.4	4.2	4.3	94%	Off-Road Vehicles	3.6	3.4	3.6	62%
Ice Skating	4.0	3.8	3.9	75%	Open Fire Allowed	3.9	4.2	4.1	71%
Kennel	4.1	3.8	4.1	62%	Playground	4.0	3.8	4.1	81%
Life Jacket	4.5	4.4	4.3	100%	Row Boating	3.8	3.8	3.7	69%
Life Preserver	3.9	3.4	3.6	76%	Sail Boating	4.1	4.0	3.9	75%

	Average Semantic Score	Average Syntactic Score	Average Pragmatic Score	To include in Standard
Skateboarding	4.3	4.2	4.1	93%
Skiing	4.6	4.2	4.5	88%
Snakes	3.7	3.5	3.6	56%
Snowmobiling	3.9	3.8	3.7	69%
Stable	3.8	3.8	3.7	73%
Swimming	4.0	3.5	3.9	67%
Swings	3.6	3.4	3.5	80%

	Average Semantic Score	Average Syntactic Score	Average Pragmatic Score	To include in Standard
Tennis	4.4	4.3	4.3	81%
Water Skiing	4.2	4.4	4.3	88%
Wind Surfing	4.4	4.3	4.4	88%

Regulatory

	Average Semantic Score	Average Syntactic Score	Average Pragmatic Score	To include in Standard
Alarm	2.6	2.3	2.1	54%
Caution Slippery	3.9	3.6	3.8	76%
Escape Stairway	2.6	3.4	2.7	50%

	Average Semantic Score	Average Syntactic Score	Average Pragmatic Score	To include in Standard			Average Semantic Score	Average Syntactic Score	Average Pragmatic Score	To include in Standard
Fire Escape	3.0	3.0	3.1	69%	No Bicycles	4.2	3.9	4.0	83%
Fire Extinguisher	4.3	4.6	4.4	94%	No Diving	4.4	4.5	4.4	82%
Fire Hose	3.1	3.0	3.0	50%	No Fishing	4.3	3.6	4.1	82%
Fire Phone	2.8	3.3	3.1	56%	No Food	4.5	3.7	4.0	75%
First Aid	4.5	4.7	4.7	94%	No Open Fire	4.3	3.9	4.2	76%
No Anchoring	4.2	3.4	3.6	76%	No Parking	4.4	4.5	4.5	74%
No Bare Feet	4.1	3.5	4.0	83%	No Pets	4.0	4.2	4.2	83%

	Average Semantic Score	Average Syntactic Score	Average Pragmatic Score	To include in Standard
No Running	4.2	3.7	4.0	84%
No Skateboarding	4.3	3.9	4.2	94%
No Smoking	4.8	4.8	4.8	100%
No Swimming	3.2	3.0	3.1	73%
No Weapons	4.3	3.9	4.0	88%
Warning	2.9	3.5	3.2	73%
Watch Step (Down)	3.2	3.7	3.5	65%

	Average Semantic Score	Average Syntactic Score	Average Pragmatic Score	To include in Standard
Watch Step (Up)	3.2	3.7	3.5	71%
Wet Floor	3.1	2.9	3.2	69%

ADA

	Average Semantic Score	Average Syntactic Score	Average Pragmatic Score	To include in Standard
Accessibility	4.4	4.5	4.5	100%
Hearing Impaired	2.6	2.9	2.8	53%
TDD	3.5	3.6	3.4	93%
Telephone Vol. Control	4.1	4.2	4.2	100%

17

Ratification

On August 21, 1995, Mayor Vera Katz held a press conference on the skybridge of World Trade Center Portland. There, she introduced the new International Pictograms Standard and unveiled the new World Trade Center Portland signage program - the first to incorporate the city's official pictograms. "Today we have raised our standard as an international city," said Katz. "We undertook this project because we agree that a picture is worth a thousand words. These pictograms will help promote our international business climate and make our city more 'user friendly' to visitors." On August 23rd, Mayor Katz introduced an ordinance to the City Council, asking them to formally adopt the International Pictograms Standard and begin implementation by replacing current signs through the regular maintenance process. The ordinance was overwhelmingly approved, and the City of Portland became the first city in the United States to formally adopt an international pictograms standard.

We had accomplished our goal! The International Pictograms Standard was established. A new awareness had been raised and steps taken to secure a more "user friendly" metropolis. Efforts to promote and encourage use of the new standard continue in Portland. A conference will be held to promote it within the metropolitan area's design community. Of even more "global" significance are plans, now being finalized, to reach out to Portland's Sister Cities around the world (currently some nine) to gain their endorsement and adoption of the standard.

Portland has every reason to be proud of this achievement. It is no less than a modern miracle when scores of municipal bureaus, agencies and private organizations come together and - in the relatively brief period of a year - produce something of worldwide value. Portland has signaled a welcome to its global neighbors. Time will tell if they choose to signal in kind.

Review and selection participants

The POVA International Subcommittee, City of Portland bureaus, agencies and organizations did not waver in their commitment to achieve the goal of creating an international pictograms standard. I would like to personally tip my hat to all those who participated in this study and acknowledge the inexhaustible effort and enormous amount of time given by everyone.

International Signage Committee

Dwyn Armstrong
Former Program Manager
Association for Portland Progress

Dian Lindsay, *Chairperson*
President
Ewe-Me & Co.

Julie Curtis
Assistant Director
Oregon Tourism Commission

Deborah Dluzen
Manager, Tourism Development
Portland Oregon Visitors Association

Mike Faha
President, Portland Chapter
American Society of Landscape Arch.

Nels Hall
Principal
Yost Grube Hall Architects

Sarah Hershey
Visitor Services Manager
Portland Oregon Visitors Association

Bill Hoffman
Manager, Pedestrian Program
Transp. & Eng., City of Portland

Val Hubbard
Former Manager, Footwear Division
Nike

Kendall Austin
Aviation Marketing Manager, Passenger
Port of Portland

Sharyl Parker
Director of Marketing
Oregon Restaurant Association

Phil Peach
Executive Director
Oregon Lodging Association

Todd Pierce, *Project Designer/Developer*
President
Design Pacifica International, LLC

Warren Schlegal
Graphic Designer
Tri-Met

Ruth Selid
City Planner
Bureau of Planning, City of Portland

Jeff Smith
Past President, Portland Chapter
American Institute of Graphic Arts

Saundra Stevens
Executive Vice President, Portland Chapt.
American Institute of Architects

Dwight Trahin
Manager, Leasing & Administration
World Trade Center Portland

Janice Larson
Creative Services Supervisor
METRO

Allyn Schroeder
Account Executive
Riddle Press

Andrew Haruyama, *Project Director*
Director
Office of International Relations
City of Portland

Robin White
Executive Vice President, Portland Chapter
Building Owners & Managers Association

Jim DiFrancesca
Assistant
Office of International Relations,
City of Portland

Bureaus of the City of Portland

Jeffery L. Rogers
City Attorney
City Attorney's Office

Margaret M. Mahoney
Director
Bureau of Buildings

David Olson
Director
Office of Cable Communications

Marcia Douglas
Education Liaison
City-School Liaison Office

Steve Rudman
Director
Bureau of Housing and
Community Development

Susan Anderson
Director
Energy Office

Dean Marriott
Director
Bureau of Environmental Services

Stephen C. Bauer
Director
Office of Finance and Administration

Robert Wall
Chief, Fire Chief's Office
Fire Bureau

David O. Kish
Director
Bureau of General Services

Shan G. Topiwalla
Manager
Computer Services Division

Marge Kafoury
Director
Office of Government Relations

Sherrill Whittemore
Acting Director
Bureau of Emergency
Communications

Frank Galida
Supervising Engineer
Hydroelectric Power

Dennis Nelson
Manager
Bureau of Licenses

Carlton Chayer
Purchasing Agent
Bureau of Purchases

John (Toby) Widmer
Director
Bureau of Maintenance

Fred Cuthbertson
Risk Manager
Risk Management Division

Helen Cheek
Director
Metropolitan Human Rights
Commission

Goran Sparrman
Director
Bureau of Traffic Management

Diane Linn
Director
Office of Neighborhood
Associations

Charles Jordan
Director
Bureau of Parks and Recreation

Kirk Berger
Personnel Director
Bureau of Personnel Services

David C. Knowles
Interim Director
Bureau of Planning

Charles Moose
Chief
Bureau of Police

Jan Burreson
Executive Director
Portland Development Commission

Becky Wehrli
Director
Portland/Multnomah Commission
on Aging

Felicia Trader
Director
Office of Transportation

Victor F. Rhodes
City Engineer/Bureau Manager
Bureau of Transportation Engineering

Mike Rosenberger
Administrator
Water Bureau

Other Contributors

Lewis & Clark College
International Student Office
Greg Caldwell, Director

The International Students of
Lewis & Clark College,
International Pictograms Study Group

Port of Portland
Taiwan Office

Port of Portland
Korea Office

Port of Portland
Tokyo Office

Port of Portland
Barbara LaBrosse
Terminal Manager

Design Pacifica International project team:
Todd Pierce, Jason West, Barbara Pierce,
Phil Davis, R.D. Aikins

Creating A Worldwide Standard
Chapter 3

A "living standard"

We now come to our major challenge: To create a dynamic, worldwide study of The International Pictograms. We want to keep the Standard as flexible as possible. To be useful over the long term, it must become a "living standard," one that changes as user needs change.

To meet the challenge, Design Pacifica International has launched a multimedia campaign to promote international awareness, distribution and participation. The book, with first-edition printing in English and Spanish, is a key element in that campaign. Plans call for future printings in additional languages.

To reach as many people as possible around the world, we have also created an interactive CD ROM (cross-platform, Macintosh and Windows). It allows users to read *PictoFacts* (History of Pictograms, How to use pictograms); enter *PictoView* (for views of pictograms by category, and more); read about the Portland Project, and become aware of pertaining ADA sign compliance issues. The CD also contains digitally-prepared illustrations of the pictograms, along with *PictoFont* (a TrueType pictogram font created by Design Pacifica International).

To encourage worldwide participation, both the book and CD ROM packages include scoring/evaluation sheets. Anyone who completes and returns a scoring form will receive a free gift in return.

The World Wide Web: http://www.pictograms.com

Global visitors may stop by our web-site on the internet to rate the effectiveness of pictograms on display. As we continue our search for new pictogram/messages to keep our Standard user-friendly, we will periodically "post" current candidates for scoring. The results will be automatically e-mailed back to our offices. These will, in turn, be compiled into fresh data for regular updates every 30 months in the form of additional books and CD ROMs.

You can participate

Our bid for ongoing global participation makes The International Pictograms Standard unique. Many symbol sets have been developed and studied by various committees and organizations around the world. Others have been designed by individuals working under temporary grants. This is the first to seek both continuous and worldwide input.

The following page is your personal scoring sheet. Please follow the instructions carefully, remove the completed form and put it in the mail. Our computer database will tabulate responses. This is your opportunity to participate in an international forum. We look forward to your reply.

The International Pictograms Standard Scoring Form

Worldwide Study

Scoring Instructions

...ncourage your participation in our ongoing Worldwide study.

... on a scale of 1-5, "5" indicating the highest degree of ...iveness, "1" the least.

...is a brief definition of the three design dimensions you ...eed to score the collection. To gain a clearer ...standing of these three dimensions, read Chapter 2.

...antic: the relationship of the visual image to the meaning.
...tactic: the relationship of one visual image to another.
...gmatic: the relationship of a visual image to the user.

...k you in advance for your participation in the first-ever ...dwide Study of The International Pictograms Standard.

Tell us about yourself

...e: _____

...pany: _____

...ress: _____

...phone: _____ e-mail: _____

...scored: _____

...ession: ❏ Architecture ❏ Graphic Design ❏ Sign Co.
...overnment Agency ❏ Other: _____

...to: The International Pictograms Standard
725 NW Flanders
Portland, OR 97209

	Semantic	Syntactic	Pragmatic
Transportation			
Agriculture			
Air Transportation			
Arriving Flights			
Baggage Check-in			
Baggage Lockers			
Bus			
Car Rental			
Customs			
Departing Flights			
Flight Information			
Gas Station			
Ground Transportation			
Heliport			
Immigration			
Moving Walkway			
Rail Transportation			
Taxi			
Ticket Purchase			
Tools			
Truck			
Tunnel			
Water Transportation			
Services			
ATM			
Bar			
Barber Shop/Salon			
Cashier			
Changing Room			
Coffee Shop			
Crosswalk			
Currency Exchange			
Dancing			
Drinking Fountain			
Falling Rocks			
Fax Machine			
Florist			
Ice Cream			
Information			
Laundry			
Leashed Pets			
Litter Disposal			
Lost & Found			
Mail			
Movie Theater			
Nursery			
Parking			
Pharmacy			
Playroom			
Public Health			
Restaurant			
Shoe Shine			
Shops			
Smoking			
Snacks			
Stroller			

	Semantic	Syntactic	Pragmatic
Telephone			
Theater/Performing Arts			
Toilets (Men)			
Toilets (Unisex)			
Toilets (Women)			
TV/Waiting Room			
Direction			
Arrow (Down & Left)			
Arrow (Down & Right)			
Arrow (Down)			
Arrow (Left)			
Arrow (Right)			
Arrow (Up & Left)			
Arrow (Up & Right)			
Arrow (Up)			
Elevator			
Entry			
Escalator			
Escalator (Down)			
Escalator (Up)			
No Entry			
Stairs			
Stairs (Down)			
Stairs (Up)			
Lodging			
Bedroom			
Bellman			
Check-in Registration			
Conference Room			
Drinking Water			
Electrical Outlet			
Hotel			
Hotel Information			
Housekeeping			
Ice			
Keys			
Light Switch			
Quiet			
Room Key Return			
Room Service			
Shower			
Thermostat			
Used Razor Blades			
Vending Machine			
Activities			
Baseball			
Bicycle			
Boat Launch			
Canoeing			
Cross-Country Skiing			
Deer			
Diving			
Exercising			
Fishing			
Golf			

	Semantic	Syntactic	Pragmatic
Gymnasium			
Hiking Trail			
Horseback Riding			
Ice Skating			
Kennel			
Life Jacket			
Life Preserver			
Marina			
Motor Boating			
Off-Road Vehicles			
Open Fire Allowed			
Playground			
Row Boating			
Sail Boating			
Skateboarding			
Skiing			
Snakes			
Snowmobiling			
Stable			
Swimming			
Swings			
Tennis			
Water Skiing			
Wind Surfing			
Regulatory			
Alarm			
Caution Slippery			
Escape Stairway			
Fire Escape			
Fire Extinguisher			
Fire Hose			
Fire Phone			
First Aid			
No Anchoring			
No Bare Feet			
No Bicycles			
No Diving			
No Fishing			
No Food			
No Open Fire			
No Parking			
No Pets			
No Running			
No Skateboarding			
No Smoking			
No Swimming			
No Weapons			
Warning			
Watch Step (Down)			
Watch Step (Up)			
Wet Floor			
ADA			
Accessibility			
Hearing Impaired			
TDD			
Telephone Vol. Control			

El estándar internacional de pictogramas

Formulario de evaluación

Una encuesta mundial

Instrucciones de evaluación

Por favor, use una escala de 1 a 5 para evaluar la efectividad de cada una de las siguientes categoriás del diseño. El "1" representa el menor grado de efectividad, y el "5" representa el mayor. Las tres dimensiones y sus definiciones son:

- **La dimensión semántica:** la relación entre la imagen visual y el significado.
- **La dimensión sintáctica:** la relación entre una imagen visual y otra.
- **La dimensión pragmática:** la relación entre una imagen visual y el usario.

Gracias por su participación en la primera encuesta mundial del estándar internacional de pictogramas.

Datos personales

Nombre:_____

Compañía:_____

Dirección:_____

_____

Teléfono:_____ e-mail:_____

Fecha de la evaluación:_____

Profesión: ❏ Arquitectura ❏ Diseño gráfico ❏ Empresa de rotulación ❏ Gobierno ❏ Otro:_____

Mail to: The International Pictograms Standard
725 NW Flanders
Portland, OR 97209

(Escalas de evaluación: Semántica / Sintáctica / Pragmática)

Transporte

- Agricultura
- Transporte aéreo
- Llegada de vuelos
- Facturación de equipajes
- Consignas automáticas
- Autobús
- Alquiler de automóviles
- Aduana
- Salida de vuelos
- Información sobre vuelos
- Estación de gasolina
- Transporte por tierra
- Helipuerto
- Inmigración
- Pasarela mecánica
- Transporte ferroviario
- Taxi
- Venta de billetes
- Herramientas
- Camión
- Túnel
- Transporte marítimo/fluvial

Servicios

- Cajero automático
- Bar
- Peluquería/Salón de belleza
- Cajero
- Probadores
- Cafetería
- Cruce
- Cambio de moneda
- Sala de baile
- Fuente de agua potable
- Caída de rocas
- Máquina de fax
- Floristería
- Heladería
- Información
- Lavandería
- Animales sujetos con correa
- Recogida de basuras
- Objetos perdidos
- Correos/Correspondencia
- Cine
- Guardería infantil
- Aparcamiento
- Farmacia
- Sala de recreo
- Sanidad pública
- Restaurante
- Limpiabotas
- Comercios
- Sección de fumadores
- Aperitivos
- Cochecito

Teléfono / Servicios

- Teléfono
- Teatro/Artes dramáticas
- Servicios/Aseos (Hombres)
- Servicios/Aseos (Unisex)
- Servicios/Aseos (Mujeres)
- Sala de espera con televisión

Direcciones

- Flecha (Abajo y a la izquierda)
- Flecha (Abajo y a la derecha)
- Flecha (Abajo)
- Flecha (Izquierda)
- Flecha (Derecha)
- Flecha (Arriba y a la izquierda)
- Flecha (Arriba y a la derecha)
- Flecha (Arriba)
- Ascensor
- Entrada
- Escaleras mecánicas
- Escaleras mecánicas (Abajo)
- Escaleras mecánicas (Arriba)
- Prohibido el paso
- Escaleras
- Escaleras (Abajo)
- Escaleras (Arriba)

Alojamiento

- Dormitorio
- Botones
- Registro en recepción
- Sala de conferencias
- Agua potable
- Toma de corriente
- Hotel
- Información sobre hoteles
- Servicio de limpieza
- Hielo
- Llaves
- Interruptor de la luz
- Silencio
- Devolución de llaves
- Servicio de habitación
- Ducha
- Termostato
- Hojillas de afeitar usadas
- Vendedora automática

Actividades

- Béisbol
- Ciclismo
- Lanchas
- Canoas
- Esquí de fondo
- Ciervos
- Buceo
- Ejercicio
- Pesca
- Golf

(Columna derecha)

- Gimnasio
- Sendero para excursionistas
- Equitación
- Esquí sobre hielo
- Perrera
- Chaleco salvavidas
- Chaleco salvavidas
- Puerto deportivo
- Lanchas motoras
- Vehículos todoterreno
- Permitido el uso de armas de fuego
- Patio de recreo
- Remo
- Vela
- Monopatinaje
- Esquí
- Serpientes
- Motonieves
- Caballerizas
- Natación
- Columpios
- Tenis
- Esquí acuático
- Tablavela

Regulación

- Alarma
- ¡Precaución! Terreno resbaladizo
- Escalera de emergencia
- Escalera de incendios
- Extintor de incendios
- Manguera
- Teléfono de incendios
- Primeros auxilios
- Prohibido anclar
- Prohibido caminar descalzo
- Prohibido para bicicletas
- Prohibido bucear
- Prohibido pescar
- Prohibido traer alimentos
- Prohibido disparar con armas de fuego
- Prohibido aparcar
- Prohibida la entrada de animales
- Prohibido correr
- Prohibido el uso de monopatín
- Prohibido fumar
- Prohibido nadar
- Prohibida la tenencia de armas
- Aviso
- Cuidado con el escalón (abajo)
- Cuidado con el escalón (arriba)
- Suelo mojado

ADA

- Accesibilidad
- Sordos/Duros de oído
- TDD
- Control de volumen del teléfono

How to Use Pictograms
Chapter 4

Recommendations for use

Pictograms are only effective when familiar, and they only become familiar when they are consistently and universally used. Consider the stop sign. Virtually everybody on the planet recognizes it. Why? Because it is everywhere; and everywhere it is, it looks virtually the same. If the International Pictograms Standard is to become universally effective, it will have to be employed consistently all over the globe. That is the goal. To reach it, we offer the following recommendations. They are intended to ensure readability, promote public recognition and allow for flexibility with regard to specific environmental conditions and design problems.

Example of dark field with light figure

Field and figure: Although it is acceptable to use a light background and dark figure, it is advisable to display pictograms with a dark field and light figure. An optical phenomenon known as the *ona effect* suggests that a light figure tends to "visually bleed" against a dark background, making it appear larger than if the inverse occurs. A light background, on the other hand, tends to visually encompass the figure, making it appear smaller. This is true for all pictograms, but especially for sign legends.

Field and figure should remain intact whenever possible. On signs, however, it is acceptable to use only the figure, since the sign background serves as the field. When multiple pictograms are used on a single sign, field and figure should always be kept intact to distinguish each message.

Color: Dark fields should be limited to black, dark neutral colors (grays and browns), forest green, navy blue, etc. Bright colors are not recommended, since colors such as bright red, blue, and yellow are designated for Regulatory-category pictograms only.

Size: Aside from ADA sign compliance requirements, which will be discussed later in this chapter, the size of a pictogram depends on its use and location. If a pictogram is used as a sign or on a sign, it is advisable to determine size in the environment intended for installation. A 12-inch tall (field and figure) pictogram can be read optimally from approximately 100 feet, and a 6-inch pictogram can be legible from approximately 50 feet away. (These guidelines are based on The International Pictograms Standard and the average complexity of figures within the collection. Pictograms with fewer intricate figures may be read from greater distances than those with more.)

Presentation of pictograms on signs: A sign displaying a pictogram is, in most cases, sufficient to convey a message. However, it is recommended that pictograms be accompanied by messages and/or sign legends. Under no circumstances should typography be added to the pictogram field. It is suggested that messages/legends be displayed directly under or to the side of the pictogram.

ADA sign compliance issues

The Americans with Disabilities Act, signed into law in 1990, is designed to provide equal access and opportunities to all Americans with disabilities. As with most legislation, many specifics are left to interpretation. Regulations for sign compliance are among these. An overview of the sign regulations specifically pertaining to the use of pictograms follows. The information provided is an interpretation only and should not be construed as legal advice or counsel. The author and publisher assume no liability, express or implied, for any errors or omissions contained herein.

Identification of Accessible Facilities and Features: Entrances, Restrooms and Bathing Facilities

The international pictogram of accessibility must be displayed at accessible entrances if all entrances are not accessible. Directions, including the pictogram, must be displayed from inaccessible entrances to accessible ones. Similar guidelines apply to restrooms and bathing facilities.

Areas of Rescue Assistance

Areas of rescue assistance must be identified with illuminated and/or non-illuminated signs, including the international pictogram of accessibility. Instructions must be posted on how to use the area during emergencies. Inaccessible exits must be identified as such. Where all exits are not accessible, signs, including the pictogram, are required to direct visitors to areas of rescue assistance.

Public Telephones

Text telephones must be identified with the TDD pictogram. Volume control telephones must be identified by the volume control telephone pictogram. Where all telephone banks are not equipped, directions, including the appropriate pictogram, must be displayed from unequipped telephones to equipped ones.

Assisted Listening Systems

Assisted listening systems must be identified by the international pictogram for hearing loss, together with a description of the system provided.

Permanent Room Designation Signs

The use of pictograms on permanent room designation signs is optional, but where used, they must be located on a field or border of at least 6-inches in height. An equivalent Grade 2 Braille

It is not recommended to add typography in a pictogram's field.

ACCESSIBILITY

Proper use of pictogram when adding typographic legend.

Here, the pictogram of "Accessibility" appears in bright blue. Consult your local governmental regulations on proper use of color.

and tactile written description (raised at least 1/32-inch from the sign surface, with exclusively upper case characters of at least 5/8-inch cap height, but not exceeding 2-inch cap height) must be placed directly below the pictogram (with the exception of arrows) and may not intrude into the 6-inch field of the pictogram.

Further Information

The ADA legislation and guidelines (ADAAG) may be obtained from the U.S. Department of Justice at:

(voice) 1.800 514.0301
(TDD) 1.800 514.0383

The Society for Environmental Graphic Design (SEGD) has published a *White Paper* providing clarification and interpretation of the regulations with regard to ADA signage requirements. This document may be obtained from SEGD at:

(voice) 202.638.5555

or e-mail at:
SEGDoffice@aol.com

Transportation
Transporte

Agriculture	Agricultura
Air Transportation	Transporte aéreo
Arriving Flights	Llegada de vuelos
Baggage Check-In	Facturación de equipajes
Baggage Lockers	Consignas automáticas
Bus	Autobús
Car Rental	Alquiler de automóviles
Customs	Aduana
Departing Flights	Salida de vuelos
Flight Information	Información sobre vuelos
Gas Station	Estación de gasolina
Ground Transportation	Transporte por tierra
Heliport	Helipuerto
Immigration	Inmigración
Moving Walkway	Pasarela mecánica
Rail Transportation	Transporte ferroviario
Taxi	Taxi
Ticket Purchase	Venta de billetes
Tools	Herramientas
Truck	Camión
Tunnel	Túnel
Water Transportation	Transporte marítimo/fluvial

Agriculture   **Agricultura**

Air Transportation   **Transporte aéreo**

Arriving Flights   **Llegada de vuelos**

Baggage Check-in   **Facturación de equipajes**

Baggage Lockers

Consignas automáticas

Bus   **Autobús**

Car Rental

Alquiler de automóviles

Customs   **Aduana**

Departing Flights   **Salida de vuelos**

Flight Information

Información sobre vuelos

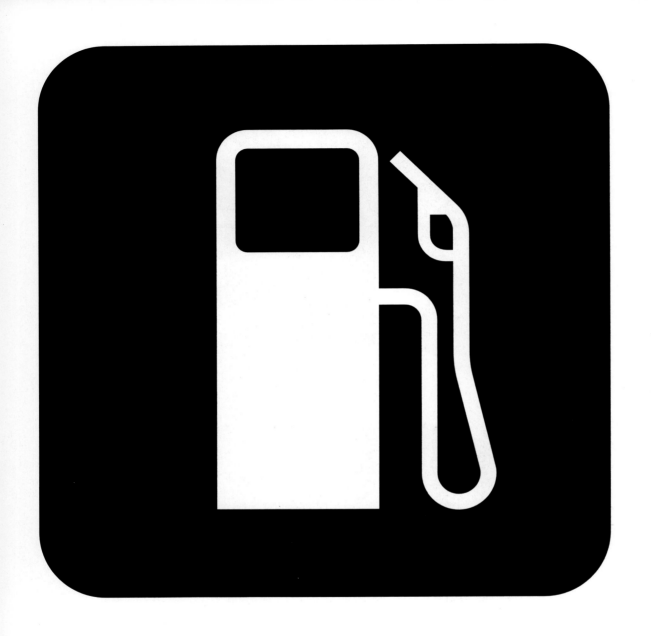

Gas Station   **Estación de gasolina**

**Ground
Transportation**

Transporte por tierra

41

Helicopter   **Helipuerto**

Immigration   **Inmigración**

Moving Walkway   **Pasarela mecánica**

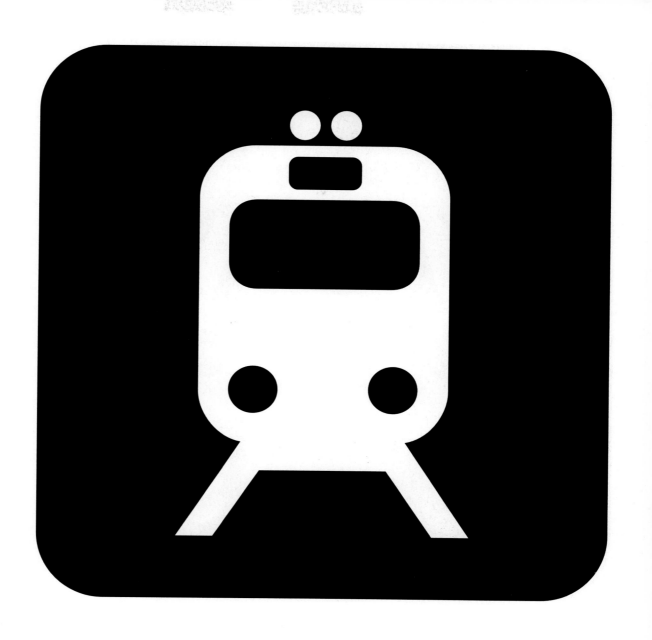

Rail Transportation   **Transporte ferroviario**

Taxi **Taxi**

Ticket purchase   **Venta de billetes**

Tools   **Herramientas**

Truck   **Camión**

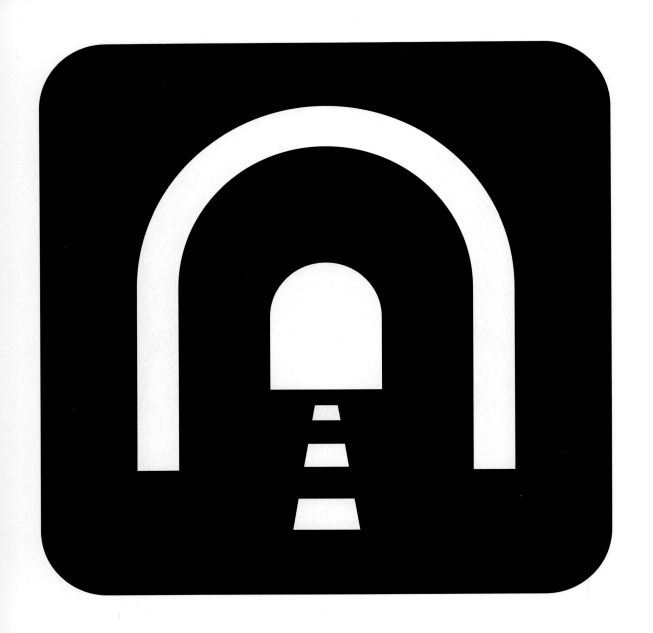

Tunnel   **Túnel**

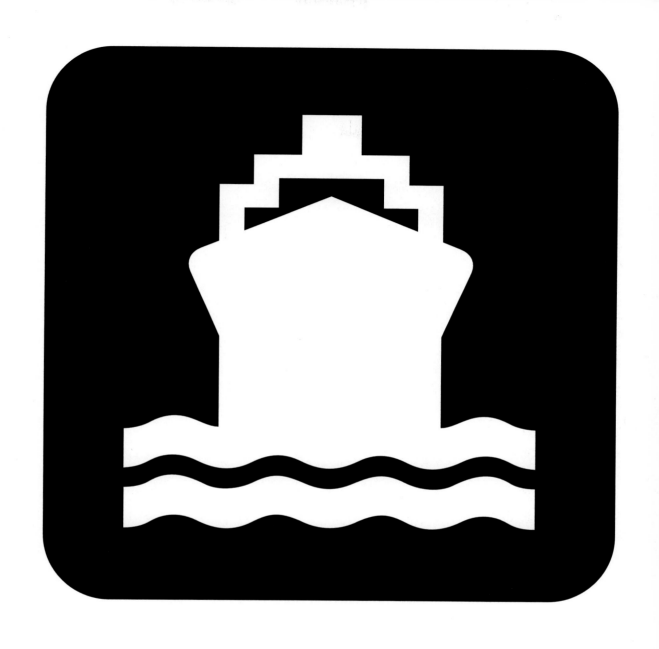

Water Transportation   Transporte marítimo/fluvial

Services
Servicios

ATM	Cajero automático
Bar	Bar
Barber Shop/Salon	Peluquería/Salón de belleza
Cashier	Cajero
Changing Rooms	Probadores
Coffee Shop	Cafetería
Crosswalk	Cruce
Currency Exchange	Cambio de moneda
Dancing	Sala de baile
Drinking Fountain	Fuente de agua potable
Falling Rocks	Caída de rocas
Fax Machine	Máquina de fax
Florist	Floristería
Ice Cream	Heladería
Information	Información
Laundry	Lavandería
Leashed Pets	Animales sujetos con correa
Litter Disposal	Recogida de basuras
Lost & Found	Objetos perdidos
Mail	Correos/Correspondencia
Movie Theater	Cine
Nursery	Guardería infantil
Parking	Aparcamiento
Pharmacy	Farmacia
Playroom	Sala de recreo
Public Health	Sanidad pública
Restaurant	Restaurante
Shoe Shine	Limpiabotas
Shops	Comercios
Smoking	Sección de fumadores
Snacks	Aperitivos
Stroller	Cochecito
Telephone	Teléfono
Theater/Performing Arts	Teatro/Artes dramáticas
Toilets (Men)	Servicios/Aseos (Hombres)
Toilets (Unisex)	Servicios/Aseos (Unisex)
Toilets (Women)	Servicios/Aseos (Mujeres)
TV Wait Room	Sala de espera con televisión

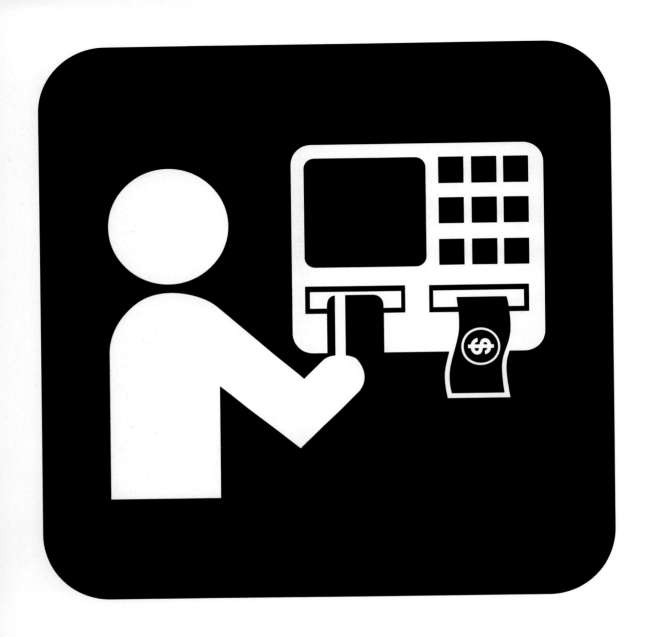

ATM   **Cajero automático**

Bar **Bar**

Baber Shop/Salon

Peluquería/Salón de belleza

Cash
Cashier

Cajero

Changing Room   **Probadores**

Coffee Shop   **Cafetería**

Crosswalk   **Cruce**

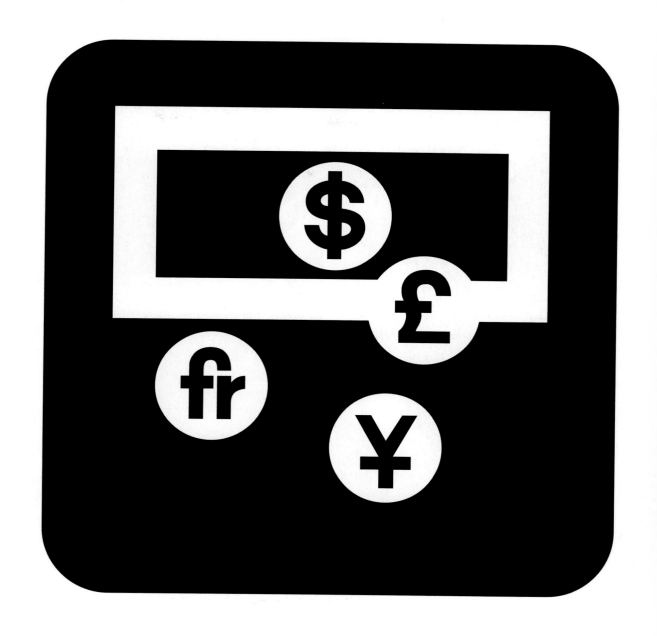

Currency Exchange　　**Cambio de moneda**

Dancing   **Sala de baile**

Drinking Fountain   **Fuente de agua potable**

Falling Rock   **Caída de rocas**

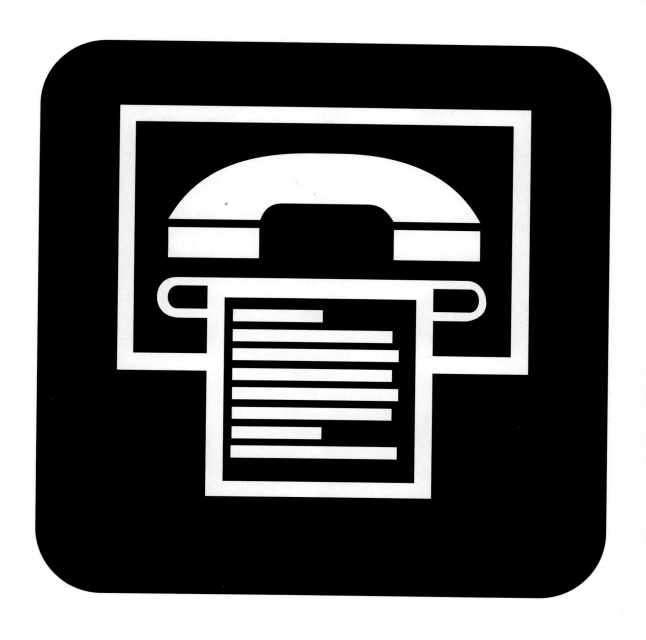

Fax   **Máquina de fax**

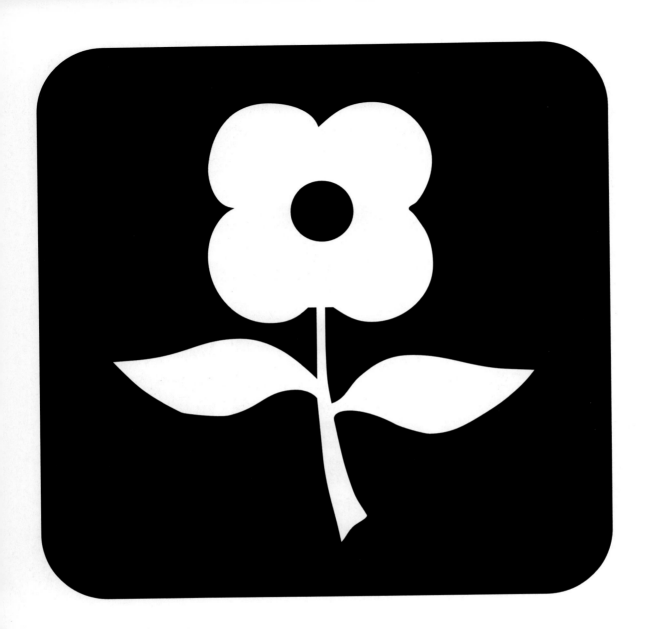

Florist   **Floristería**

Ice Cream   **Heladería**

Information   **Información**

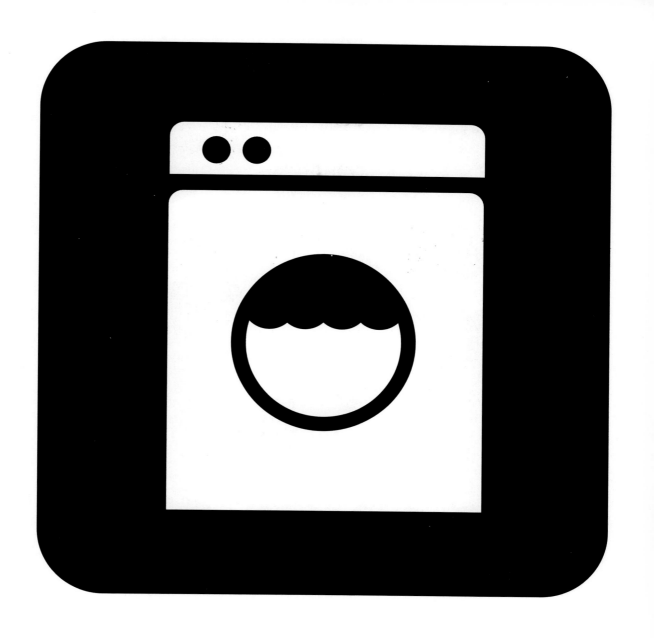

Laundry　　　　　　　　**Lavandería**

Leashed Pets

Animales sujetos con correa

Litter Disposal   **Recogida de basuras**

Lost & Found   **Objetos perdidos**

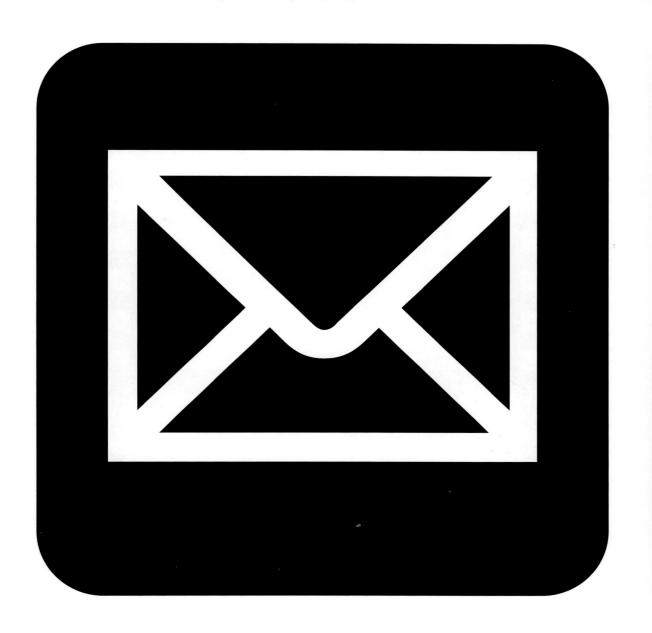

Mail

**Correos/
Correspondencia**

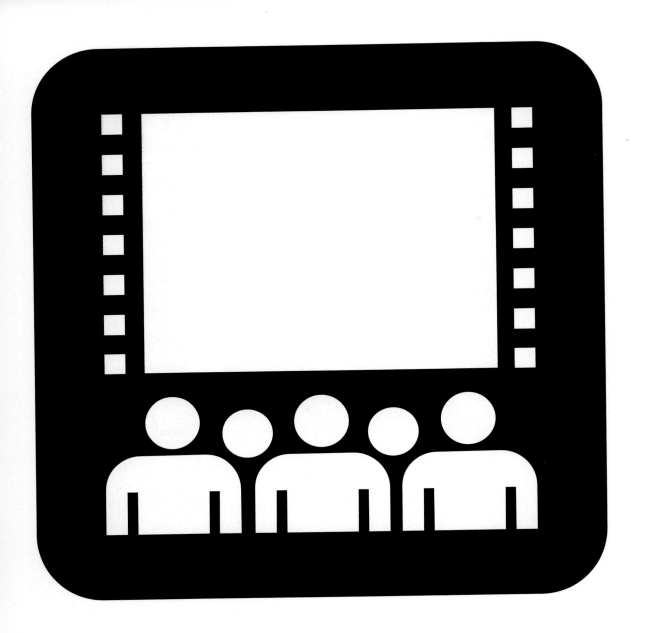

Movie Theater   **Cine**

Nursery **Guardería infantil**

Parking   **Aparcamiento**

Pharmacy　　　　　**Farmacia**

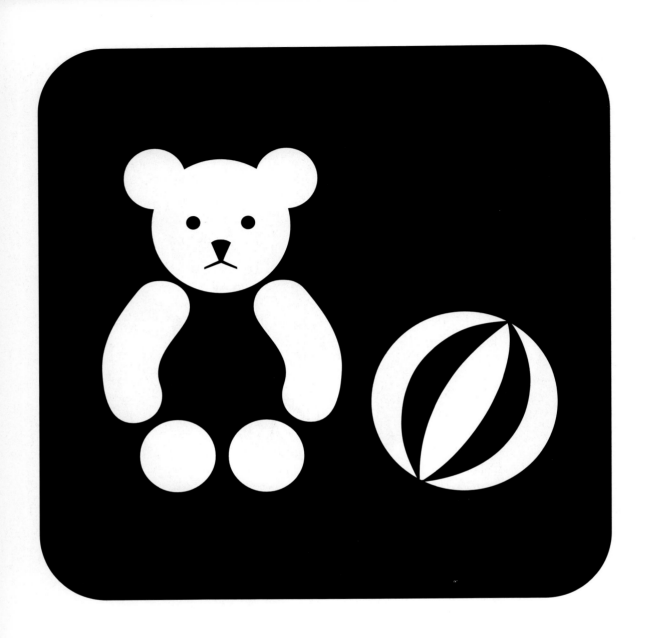

Playroom　　　　　　**Sala de recreo**

Public Health   **Sanidad pública**

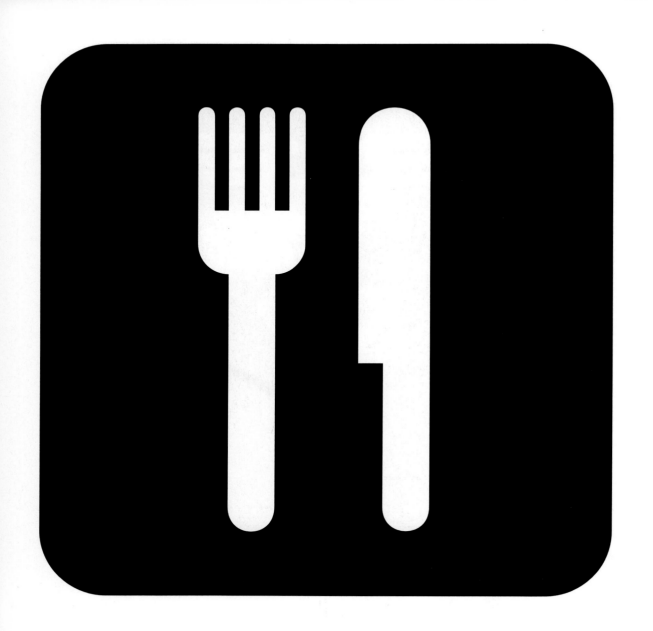

Restaurant   **Restaurante**

Shoe Shine   **Limpiabotas**

Shop   **Comercios**

Smoking   **Sección de fumadores**

Snacks   **Aperitivos**

Stroller   **Cochecito**

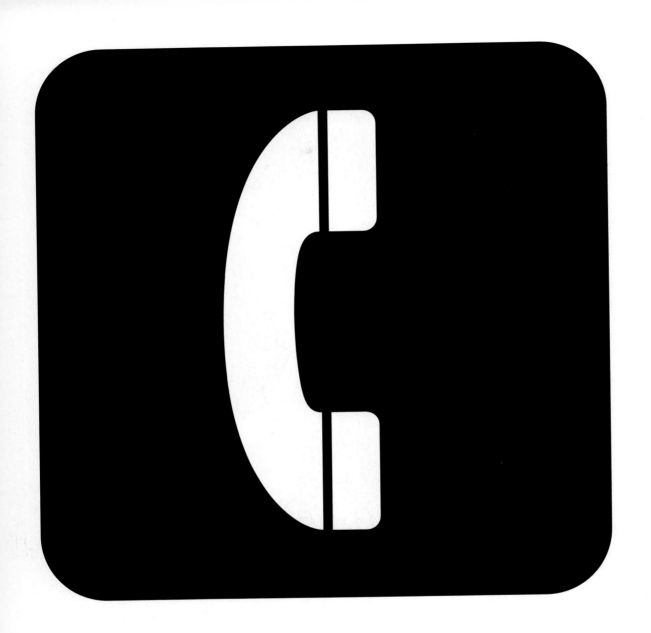

Telephone   **Teléfono**

**Theatre
Performing Arts**

**Teatro
Artes dramáticas**

**Toilets
(Men)**

**Servicios/Aseos
(Hombres)**

**Toilets
(Unisex)**

**Servicios/Aseos
(Unisex)**

**Toilets
(Women)**

**Servicios/Aseos
(Mujeres)**

TV Wait Room　　　**Sala de espera con televisión**

Direction
Direcciones

Arrow (Down & Left)	Flecha (Abajo y a la izquierda)
Arrow (Down & Right)	Flecha (Abajo y a la derecha)
Arrow (Down)	Flecha (Abajo)
Arrow (Left)	Flecha (Izquierda)
Arrow (Right)	Flecha (Derecha)
Arrow (Up & Left)	Flecha (Arriba y a la izquierda)
Arrow (Up & Right)	Flecha (Arriba y a la derecha)
Arrow (Up)	Flecha (Arriba)
Elevator	Ascensor
Entry	Entrada
Escalator	Escaleras mecánicas
Escalator (Down)	Escaleras mecánicas (Abajo)
Escalator (Up)	Escaleras mecánicas (Arriba)
No Entry	Prohibido el paso
Stairs	Escaleras
Stairs (Down)	Escaleras (Abajo)
Stairs (Up)	Escaleras (Arriba)

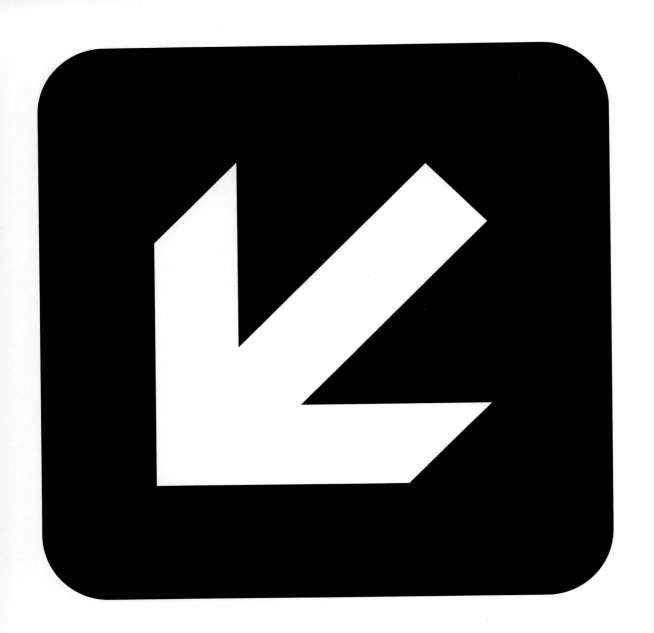

**Arrow
(Down & Left)**

**Flecha
(Abajo y a la izquierda)**

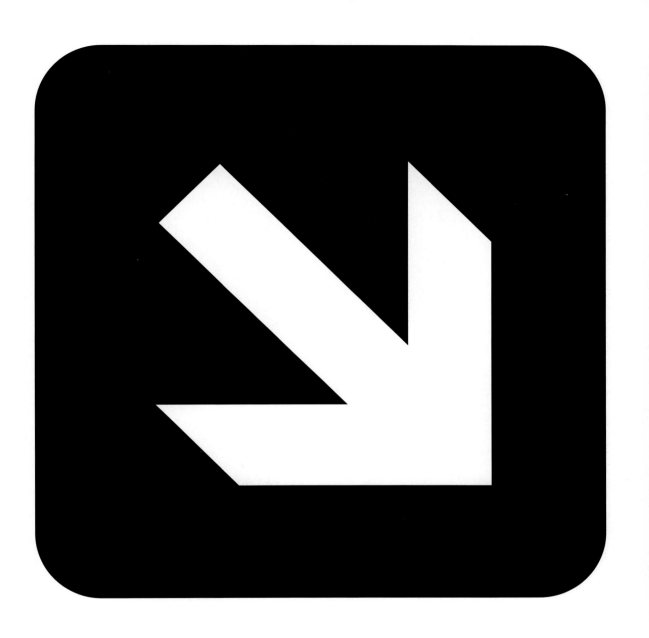

**Arrow
(Down & Right)**

**Flecha
(Abajo y a la derecha)**

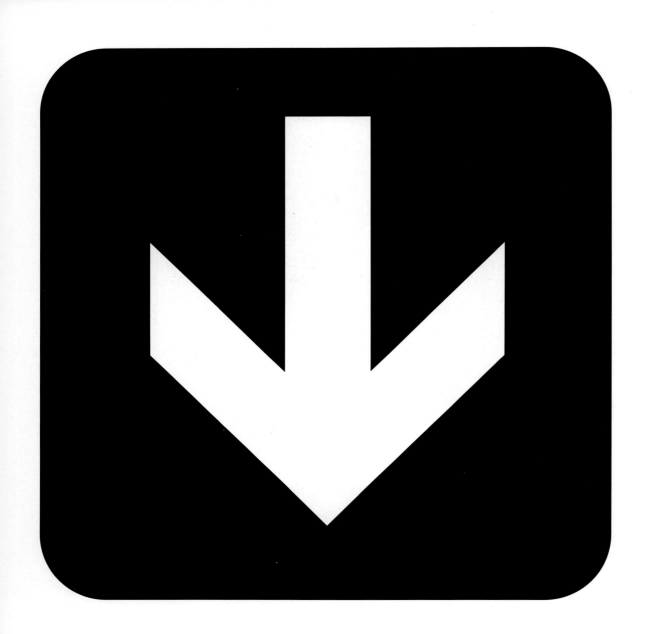

**Arrow
(Down)**

**Flecha
(Abajo)**

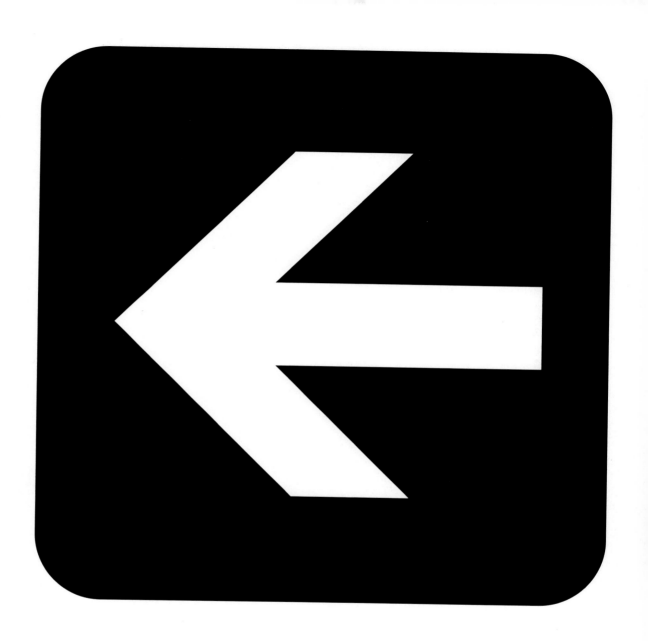

**Arrow
(Left)**

**Flecha
(Izquierda)**

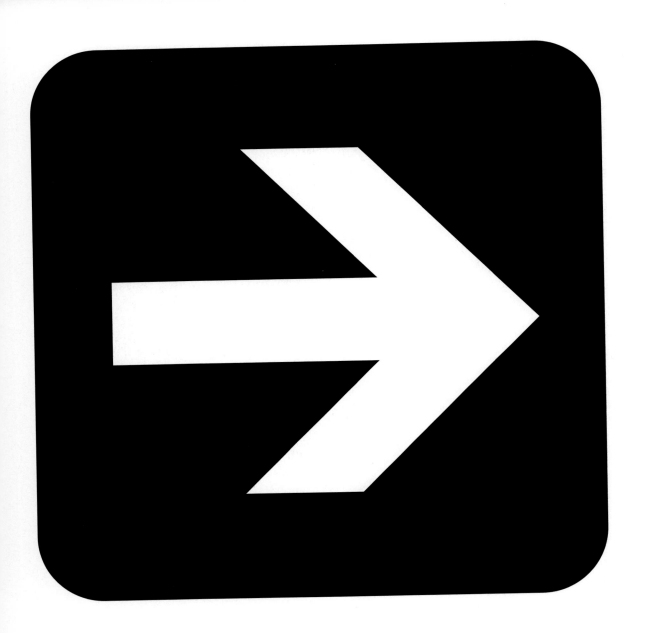

**Arrow
(Right)**

**Flecha
(Derecha)**

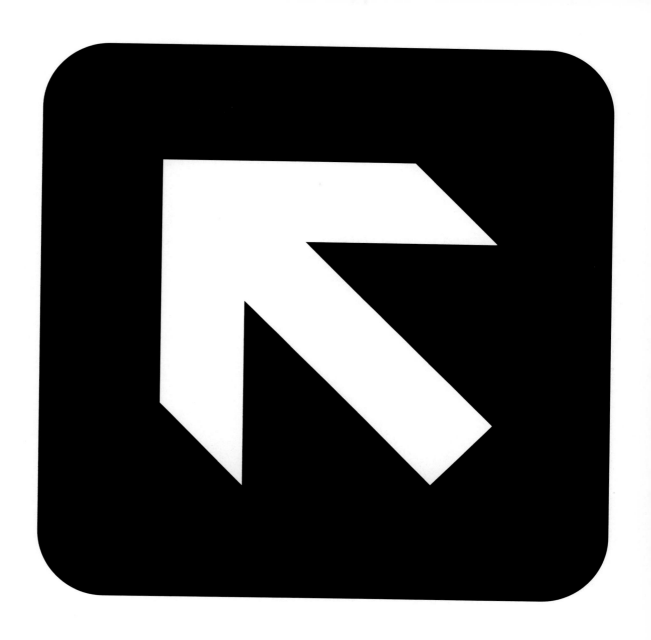

**Arrow
(Up & Left)**

**Flecha
(Arriba y a la izquierda)**

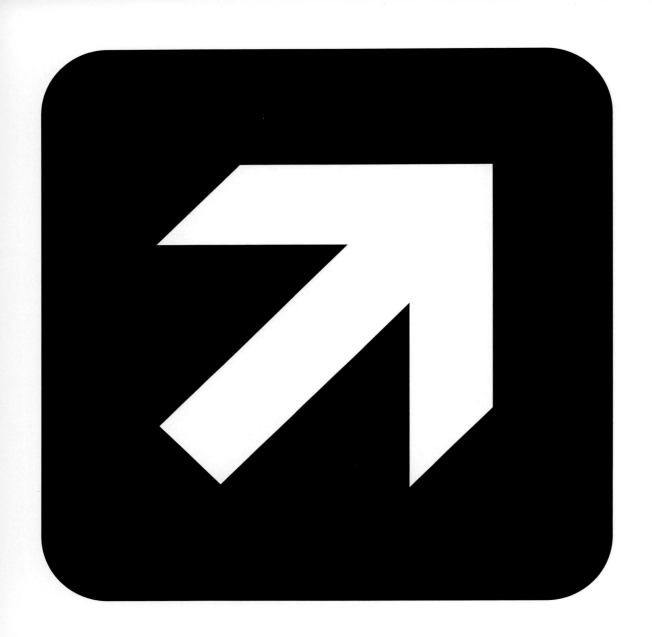

**Arrow
(Up & Right)**

**Flecha
(Arriba y a la derecha)**

**Arrow
(Up)**

**Flecha
(Arriba)**

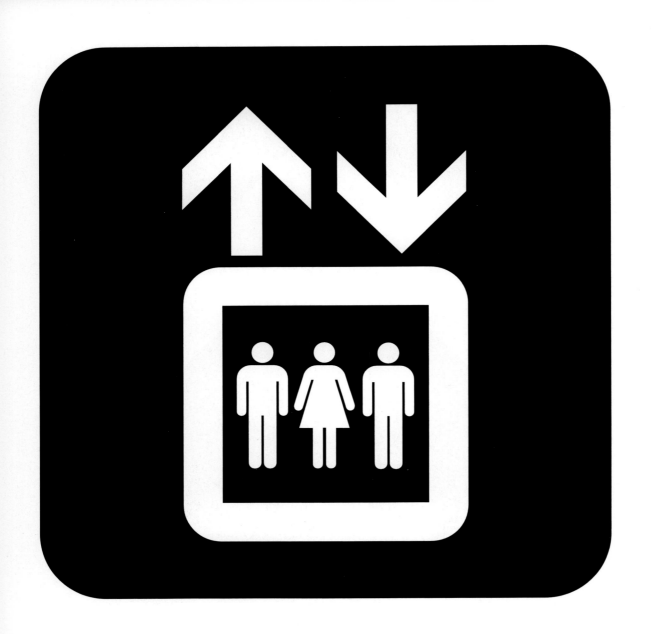

Elevator   **Ascensor**

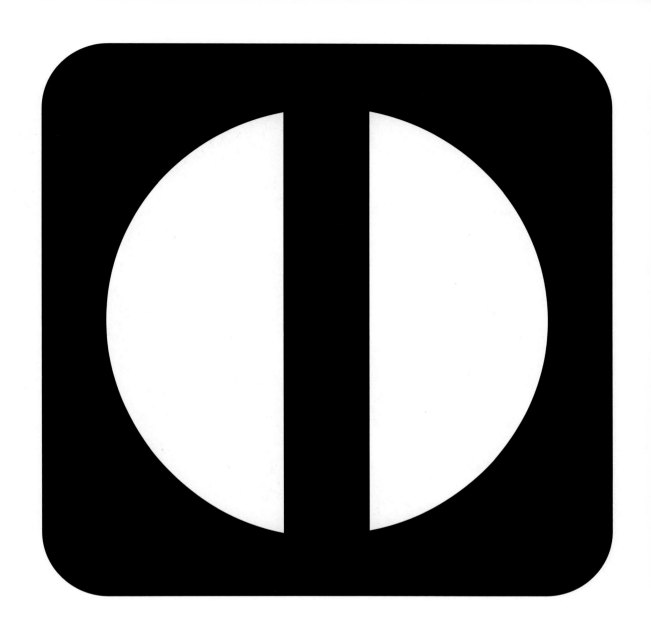

Entry   **Entrada**

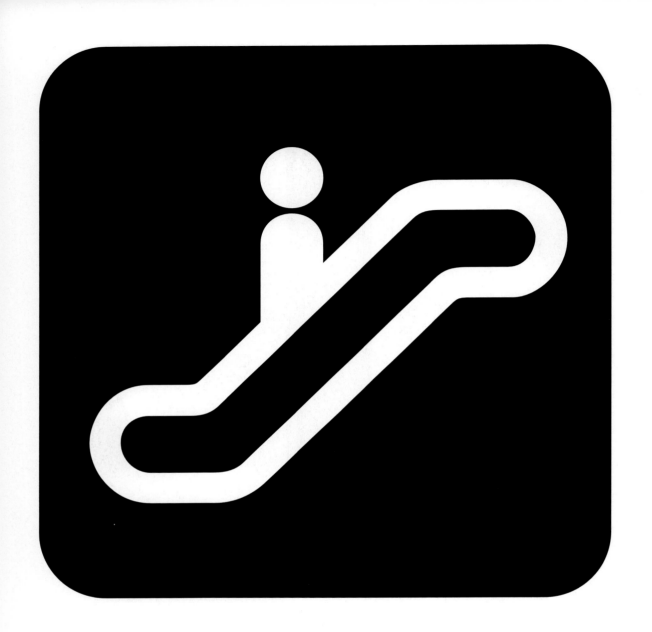

Escalator   **Escaleras mecánicas**

**Escalator
(Down)**

**Escaleras mecánicas
(Abajo)**

**Escalator
(Up)**

**Escaleras mecánicas
(Arriba)**

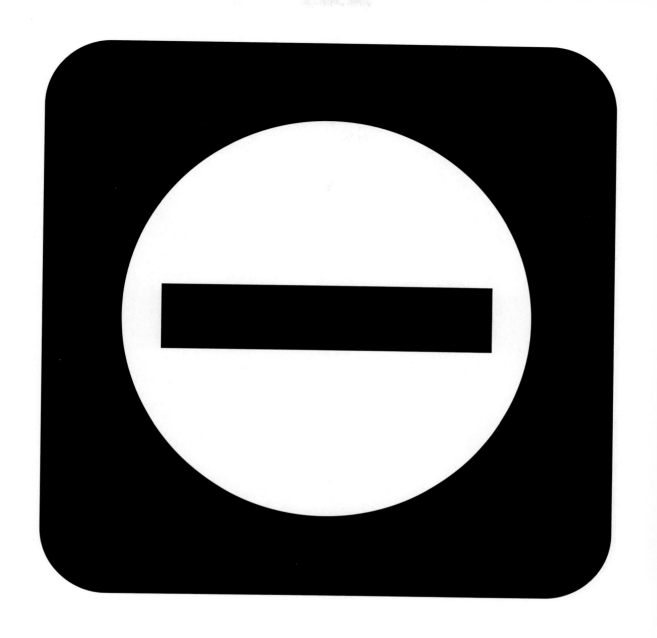

No Entry   **Prohibido el paso**

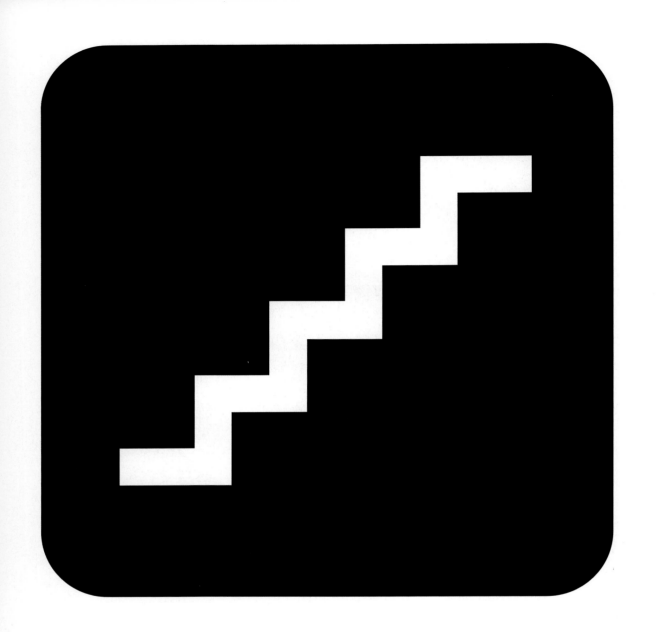

Stairs　　　　　　　**Escaleras**

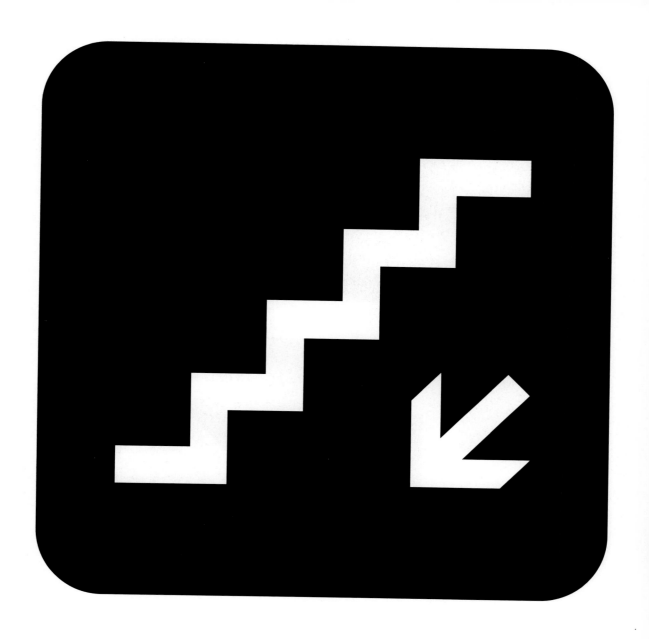

**Stairs
(Down)**

**Escaleras
(Abajo)**

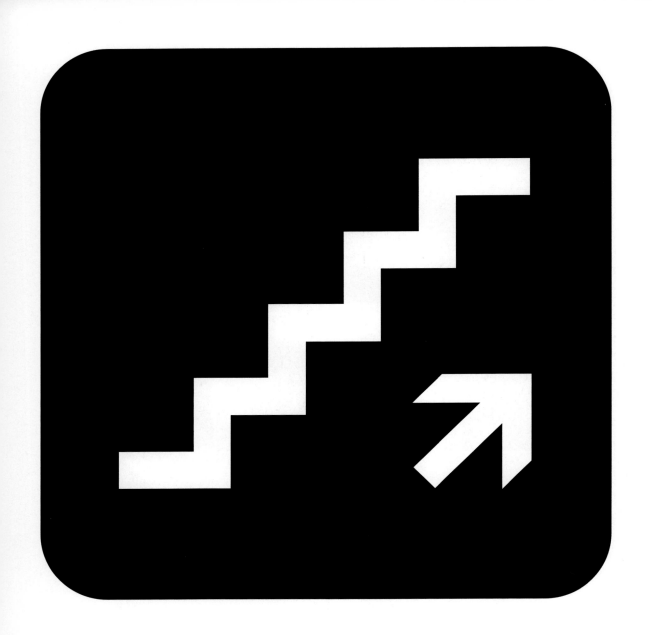

**Stairs
(Up)**

**Escaleras
(Arriba)**

Lodging
Alojamiento

Bedroom	Dormitorio
Bellman	Botones
Check-In Registration	Inscripción/registro en recepción
Conference Room	Sala de conferencias
Drinking Water	Agua potable
Electrical Outlet	Toma de corriente
Hotel	Hotel
Hotel Information	Información sobre hoteles
Housekeeping	Servicio de limpieza
Ice	Hielo
Keys	Llaves
Light Switch	Interruptor de la luz
Quiet	Silencio
Room Key Return	Devolución de llaves
Room Service	Servicio de habitación
Shower	Ducha
Thermostat	Termostato
Used Razor Blades	Hojillas de afeitar usadas
Vending Machine	Vendedora automática [expendedor]

Bedroom   **Dormitorio**

Bellman   **Botones**

Check-in Registration   **Inscripción/registro en recepción**

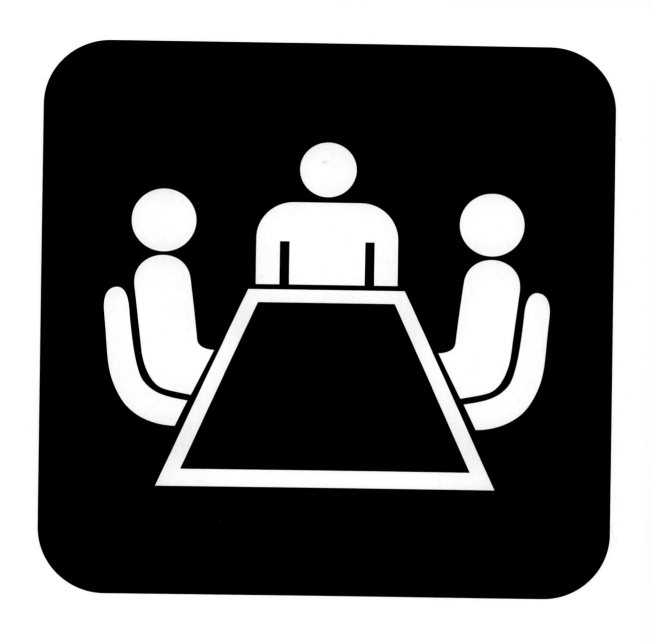

Conference Room   **Sala de conferencias**

Drinking Water   **Agua potable**

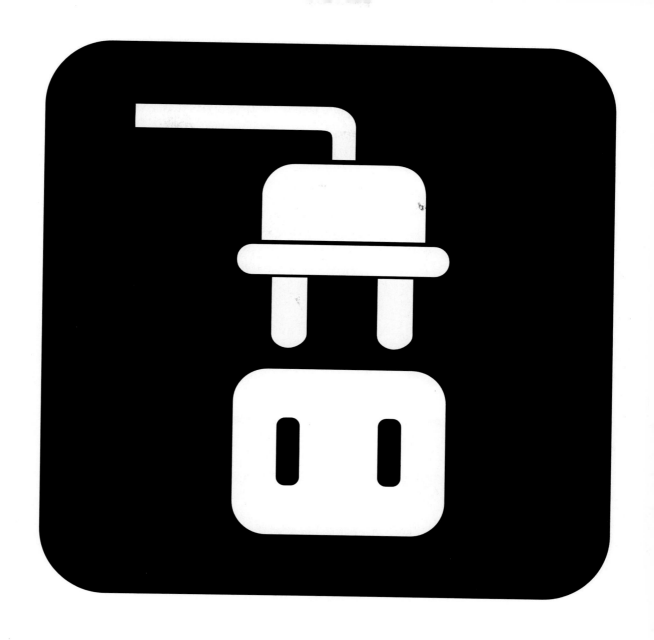

Electrical Outlet   **Toma de corriente**

Hotel   **Hotel**

Hotel Information

Información sobre hoteles

House Keeping   **Servicio de limpieza**

Ice **Hielo**

Keys   **Llaves**

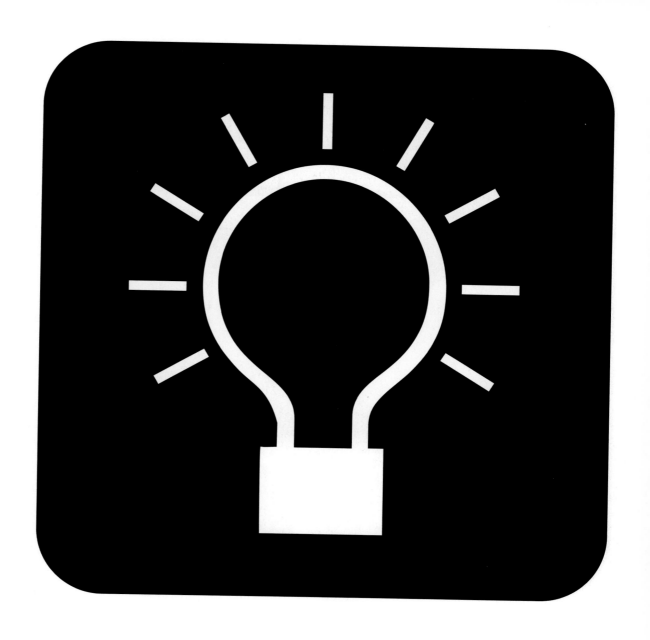

Light Switch   **Interruptor de la luz**

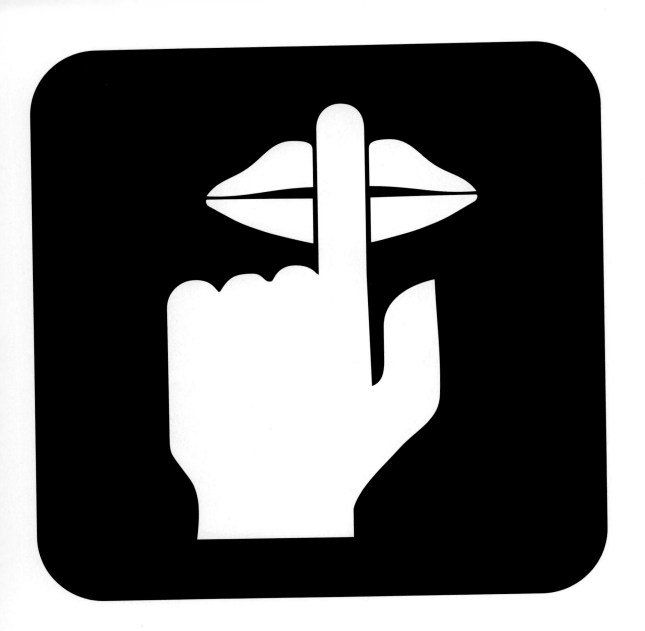

Quiet　　　　　　　**Silencio**

Room Key Return   **Devolución de llaves**

Room Service

Servicio de habitación

Shower   **Ducha**

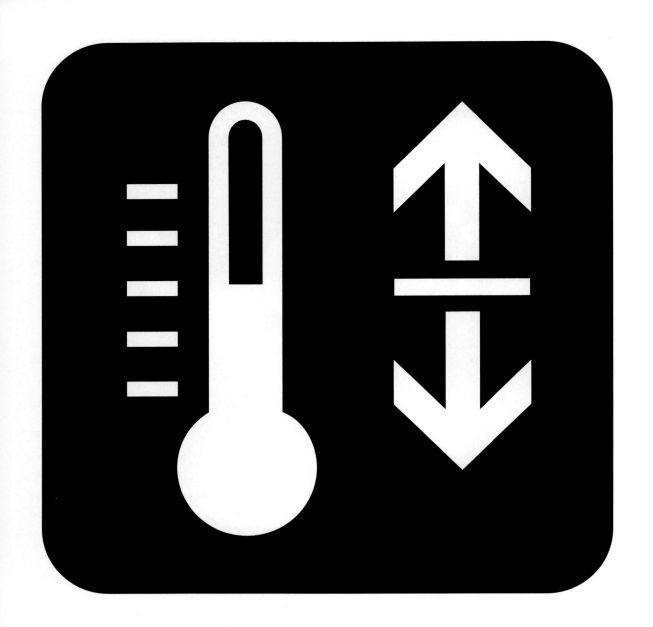

Thermostat   **Termostato**

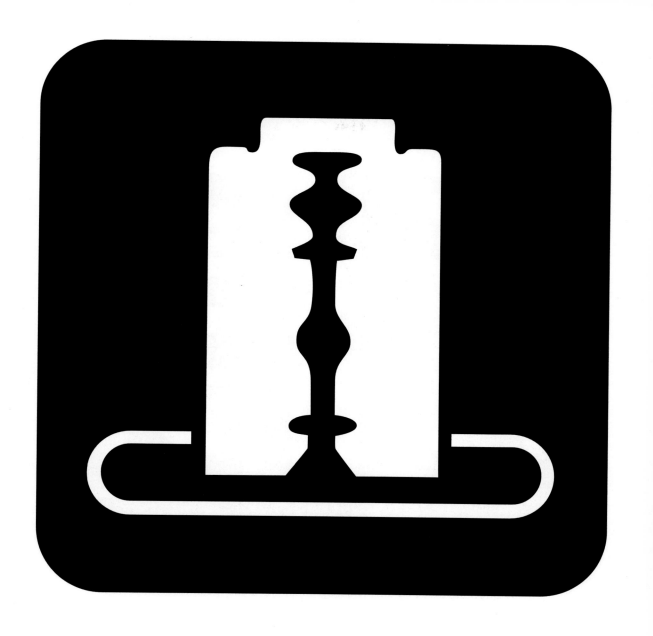

Used Razor Blades   **Hojillas de afeitar usadas**

Vending Machines

Vendedora automática [expendedor]

Activities
Actividades

Baseball	Béisbol
Bicycle	Ciclismo
Boat Launch	Lanchas
Canoeing	Canoas
Cross-Country Skiing	Esquí de fondo
Deer	Ciervos
Diving	Buceo
Exercising	Ejercicio
Fishing	Pesca
Golf	Golf
Gymnasium	Gimnasio
Hiking Trail	Sendero para excursionistas
Horseback Riding	Equitación
Ice Skating	Esquí sobre hielo
Kennel	Perrera
Life Jacket	Chaleco salvavidas
Life Preserver	Chaleco salvavidas
Marina	Puerto deportivo
Motor Boating	Lanchas motoras
Off-Road Vehicles	Vehículos todoterreno
Open Fire Allowed	Permitido el uso de armas de fuego
Playground	Patio de recreo
Row Boating	Remo
Sail Boating	Vela
Skateboarding	Monopatinaje
Skiing	Esquí
Snakes	Serpientes
Snowmobiling	Motonieves
Stable	Caballerizas
Swimming	Natación
Swings	Columpios
Tennis	Tenis
Water Skiing	Esquí acuático
Wind Surfing	Tablavela

Baseball   **Béisbol**

Bicycle   **Ciclismo**

Boat Launch   **Lanchas**

Canoeing   **Canoas**

Cross Country Skiing

Esquí de fondo

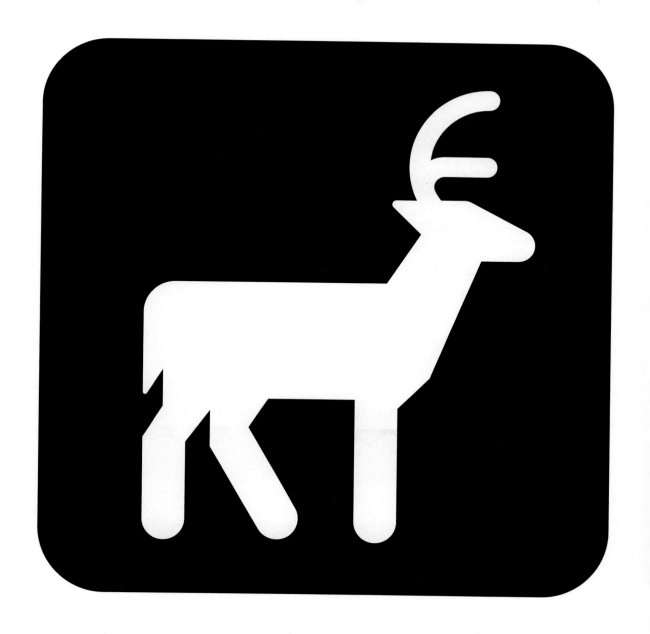

Deer   **Ciervos**

Diving   **Buceo**

Exercising   **Ejercicio**

139

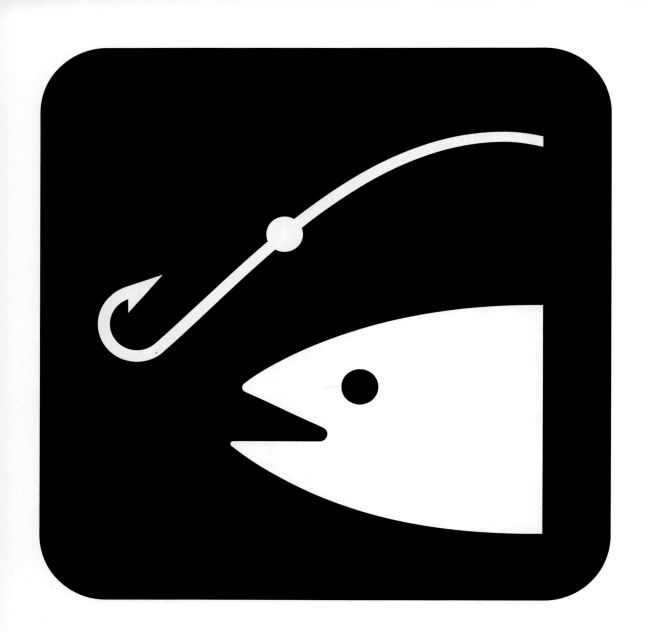

Fishing　　　　　　　**Pesca**

Golf   **Golf**

141

Gymnasium   **Gimnasio**

Hiking Trail

Sendero para excursionistas

Horseback Riding   **Equitación**

Ice Skating   **Esquí sobre hielo**

Kennel   **Perrera**

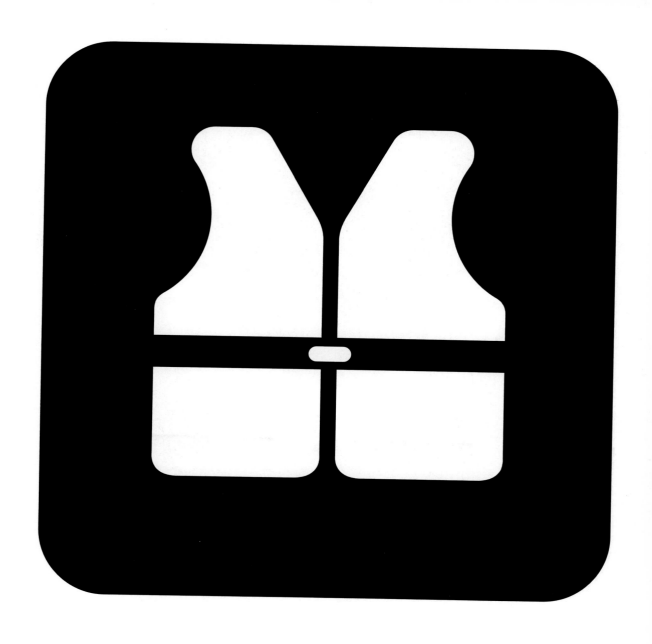

Life Jacket   **Chaleco salvavidas**

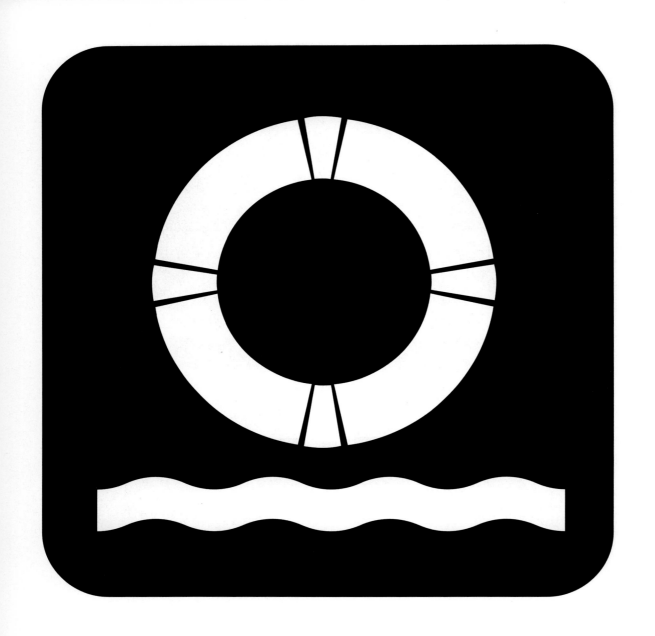

Life Preserver   **Chaleco salvavidas**

Marina   **Puerto deportivo**

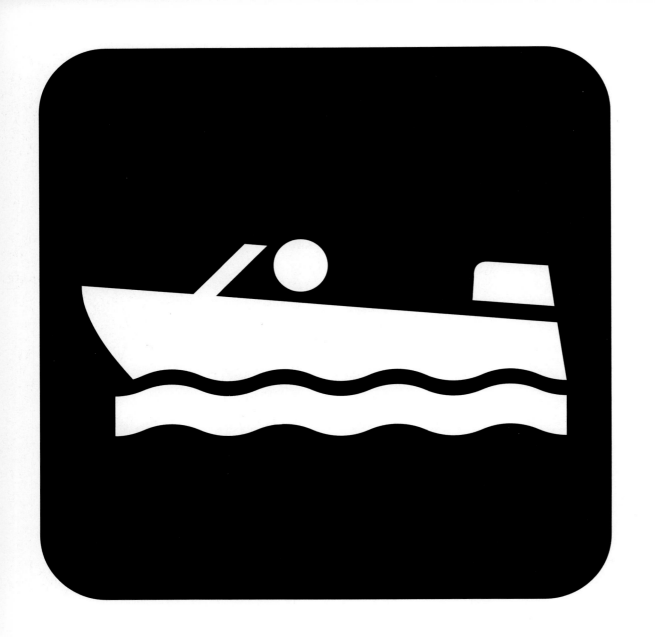

Motor Boating   **Lanchas motoras**

Off Road Vehicles

Vehículos todoterreno

Open Fire Allowed

Permitido el uso de armas de fuego

152

Playground　　　　　**Patio de recreo**

Row Boating   **Remo**

Sail Boating   **Vela**

155

Skateboarding   **Monopatinaje**

Skiing

Esquí

Snakes　　　　　　**Serpientes**

Snowmobiling   **Motonieves**

Stable   **Caballerizas**

Swimming   **Natación**

Swings   **Columpios**

Tennis   **Tenis**

Water Skiing   **Esquí acuático**

Wind Surfing   **Tablavela**

Regulatory
Regulación

Alarm	Alarma
Caution Slippery	¡Precaución! Terreno resbaladizo
Escape Stairway	Escalera de emergencia
Fire Escape	Escalera de incendios
Fire Extinguisher	Extintor de incendios
Fire Hose	Manguera
Fire Phone	Teléfono de incendios
First Aid	Primeros auxilios
No Anchoring	Prohibido anclar
No Bare Feet	Prohibido caminar descalzo
No Bicycles	Prohibido para bicicletas
No Diving	Prohibido bucear
No Fishing	Prohibido pescar
No Food	Prohibido traer alimentos
No Open Fire	Prohibido disparar con armas de fuego
No Parking	Prohibido aparcar
No Pets	Prohibida la entrada de animales
No Running	Prohibido correr
No Skateboarding	Prohibido el uso de monopatín
No Smoking	Prohibido fumar
No Swimming	Prohibido nadar
No Weapons	Prohibida la tenencia de armas
Warning	Aviso
Watch Step (Down)	Cuidado con el escalón (abajo)
Watch Step (Up)	Cuidado con el escalón (arriba)
Wet Floor	Suelo mojado

Alarm   **Alarma**

Caution Slippery

¡Precaución! Terreno resbaladizo

Escape Stairway

Escalera de emergencia

Fire Escape   **Escalera de incendios**

Fire Extinguisher   **Extintor de incendios**

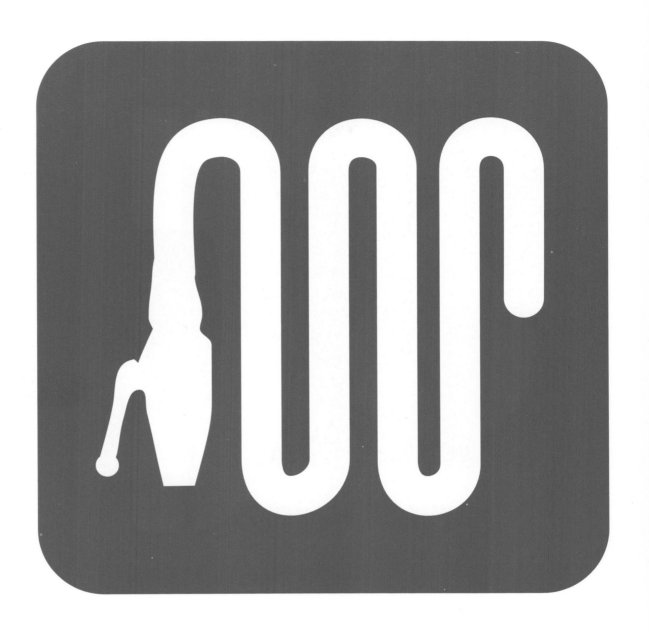

Fire Hose   **Manguera**

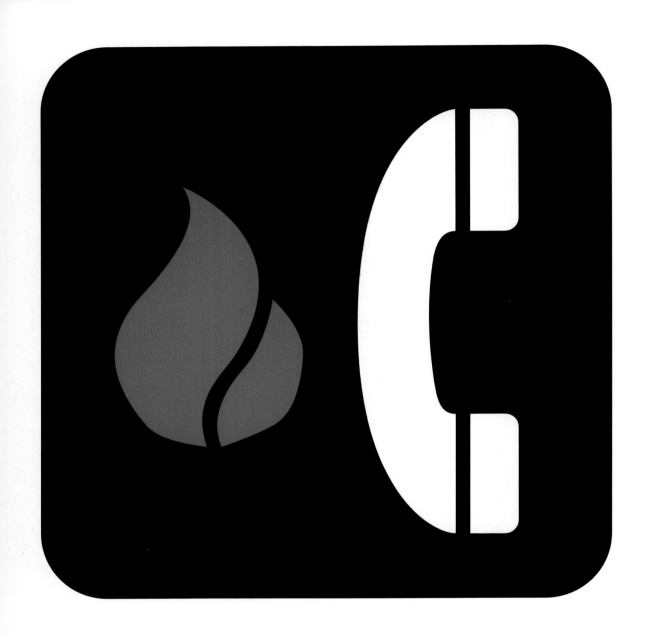

Fire Phone　　　　　　**Teléfono de incendios**

First Aid   **Primeros auxilios**

No Anchoring   **Prohibido anclar**

No Bare Feet

**Prohibido caminar
descalzo**

No Bicycle

Prohibido para bicicletas

No Diving

Prohibido bucear

No Fishing   **Prohibido pescar**

No Food

**Prohibido traer
alimentos**

No Open Fire

**Prohibido disparar
con armas de fuego**

No Parking   **Prohibido aparcar**

No Pets

Prohibida la entrada de animales

No Running   **Prohibido correr**

No Skateboarding   **Prohibido el uso de monopatín**

No Smoking   **Prohibido fumar**

No Swimming   **Prohibido nadar**

Warning

Prohibida la tenencia de armas

Warning   **Aviso**

Watch Step (Down)

Cuidado con el escalón (abajo)

Watch Step (Up)

Cuidado con el escalón (arriba)

Wet Floor   **Suelo mojado**

ADA

Accessibility
Hearing Impaired
TDD
Telephone Volume Control

Accesibilidad
Sordos/Duros de oído
TDD
Control de volumen del teléfono

Accessibility   **Accesibilidad**

Hearing Impaired   **Sordos**
Duros de oído

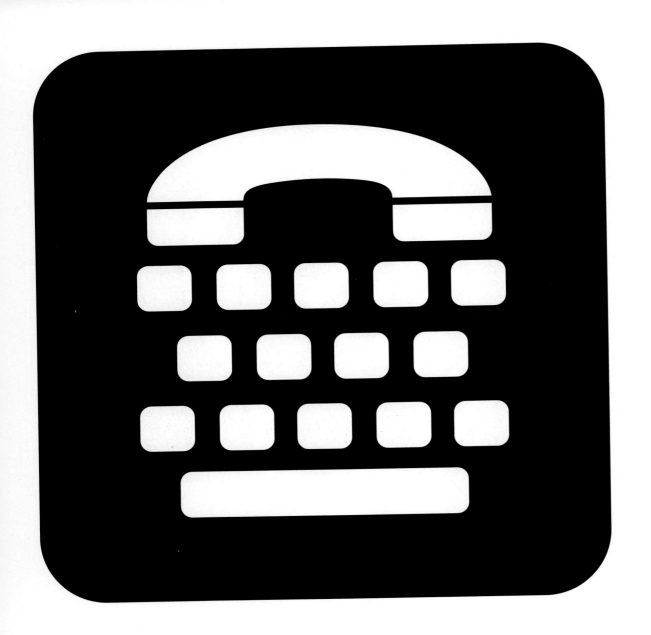

TDD   **TDD**

108

Telephone Volume Control

Control de volumen del teléfono

Spanish
en Español

El Standard Internacional de Pictogramas

Escrito y desarrollado por Todd Pierce,
Design Pacifica International, LLC
Publicado por ST Publications, Inc.

Primera edición

Esta reproducción escrita de pictogramas
está protegida por derechos de autor. Sin
embargo, los pictogramas mismos están
libres de derechos, y está permitido su uso
por la industria de comunicación visual de
todo el mundo. No se permite su
reproducción por ningún otro medio ni
para ningún otro propósito.

Para mayor información, póngase en
contacto con :

ST Publications Book Division
407 Gilbert Avenue
Cincinnati, Ohio 45202
U.S.A.

Diseño del libro: Copyright 1996, por Todd Pierce,
Design Pacifica International, LLC
Imprimido en los Estados Unidos de América

ISBN 0-944094-22-8

El Standard Internacional de Pictogramas en CD ROM

Design Pacifica International, LLC, ha puesto en circulación un CD ROM interactivo (plataforma mixta, Macintosh y Windows) que contiene material gráfico Encapsulated PostScript y PictoFont (tipos de letra TrueType para pictogramas) para cada una de las ilustraciones, al precio de 179 dólares USA. Para encargos, mande un cheque o giro postal a:

The International Pictograms Standard
725 NW Flanders
Portland, OR 97209, USA

o llame a Design Pacifica International al (503) 222.9494

correo electrónico:
tpierce@designpacifica.com

El Standard Internacional de Pictogramas en la World Wide Web

http://www.pictograms.com
correo electrónico: info@pictograms.com

INTRODUCCIÓN

Este libro trata sobre pictogramas internacionales. Hay muchas palabras que se usan para describir un pictograma -- tales como ideograma, icono, señal simbólica, pictografía, símbolo pictórico, etc. En las páginas que siguen utilizo todas indistintamente. Sin embargo, mi favorita es "pictograma". Esta palabra dice todo lo que necesita decirse. "Icono", sin embargo, tiene ciertas connotaciones religiosas. "Pictografía" también puede significar "gráfica" o "esquema". Y "símbolo" tiene varios significados. "Pictograma", en cambio, resume sencillamente la realidad que define: "picto" quiere decir imagen y "grama" mensaje, como en la palabra "telegrama". Pero no se me malentienda: éste no es un libro sobre palabras. Trata sobre algo más básico: comunicación, un medio de comunicación simplificable que todo el mundo pueda entender. Trata sobre la búsqueda de una forma de mejorar la comunicación en la metrópolis global de hoy, una forma que supere las barreras lingüísticas y simplifique los mensajes básicos.

Y algo más. Este libro describe asimismo un estudio que se llevó a cabo durante un año en Portland, Oregón. Aquí se explican los objetivos de aquel estudio, su proceso de desarrollo y los resultados que produjo. A los que trabajamos en ello, una magnífica visión nos inspiró: la de crear un estudio perpetuo. Y también un objetivo principal -- ofrecer al mundo entero un standard internacional de pictogramas. Para crearlo, pues, quisimos solicitar la ayuda de todos. Ahora volvemos a solicitarla, para mantener nuestro standard actual y "con vida".

El lector encontrará una hoja de evaluación en el interior del libro. Espero que la utilice. Por favor, sea tan amable de rellenarla y mandármela por correo. Su aportación no será tan sólo bien acogida, sino tratada como algo fundamental. Para que un standard alcance status mundial, es preciso que tenga más de un autor. El Standard Internacional de Pictogramas queda abierto a la participación, aportación y mejoras de todos.

¡Espero con interés su opinión! Ojalá que disfrute del libro.

Todd Pierce
Presidente
Design Pacifica International, LLC

203

HISTORIA DE LOS PICTOGRAMAS

Formas primitivas de comunicación

El recurso humano a los símbolos pictóricos o pictogramas, como frecuentemente se les llama hoy, se remonta hasta las señales prehistóricas inscritas en la roca y paredes de las cuevas. Ya en el año 2000 antes de Cristo, los egipcios habían creado imágenes simplificadas que eventualmente llevarían a la sustitución de las imágenes simbólicas por una escritura fonética. En el transcurso de los siglos, las lenguas evolucionaron y aportaron una enorme variedad al proceso de la comunicación. Con más de cien lenguas y seis mil dialectos actualmente en el mundo, la comunicación internacional se ha complicado abrumadoramente.

En los últimos trescientos años, se han realizado varios intentos de crear un método de comunicación universal mediante la vuelta a las simples imágenes simbólicas usadas por el hombre primitivo. Innovaciones tales como los símbolos del Sistema Internacional de Educación por Imágenes Tipográficas (International System of Typographic Picture Education, ISOTYPE), inventado por Otto Neurath en los años veinte, y los Símbolos de Semantografía diseñados por Charles Bliss durante los cuarenta, han inspirado una confianza general en que el simbolismo es la mejor y más efectiva herramienta para transmitir y recibir información a nivel internacional.

El estudio de señales simbólicas AIGA/D.O.T. de 1974

Ya en la década de los setenta, se usaban en todo el mundo veintiocho conjuntos diferentes de pictogramas. Sin embargo, ninguno de ellos respondía a un criterio globalizador que fuera tan consistente como apropiado para merecer su reconocimiento internacional. En 1974, por encargo del Departamento de Transporte de los EEUU (D.O.T), y con el apoyo de una beca de la Fundación Nacional para las Artes (National Endowment for the Arts), el Instituto Americano de Artes Gráficas (American Institute of Graphic Arts, AIGA) creó un comité para desarrollar un conjunto de símbolos único, uniformizado y reconocido internacionalmente. El comité AIGA, encabezado por Thomas H. Geimar, desarrolló una serie de criterios para evaluar los conjuntos de pictogramas existentes. El objetivo era establecer una colección de símbolos consistente e interrelacionada que pudiera superar las barreras lingüísticas y simplificar mensajes básicos para el área de transporte en todo el mundo. Gracias a una promoción masiva, así como a su uso y aceptación, este conjunto standard de señales se ha convertido hoy en el grupo de pictogramas más utilizado del mundo.

Pictogramas para una metrópolis "global"

Aún así, el conjunto D.O.T. de señales simbólicas, enfocado principalmente en mensajes relacionados con el transporte, sirve para un propósito limitado. En los últimos veinte años, organizaciones de todo el mundo se han esforzado por crear conjuntos standard adicionales.

Tres de ellos son especialmente dignos de mención. En 1985, el Cuerpo de Ingenieros del Ejército de Tierra americano, bajo la dirección de diseño de Don Meeker, desarrolló una serie de símbolos para actividades recreativas nacionales, a ser utilizados por el Servicio Nacional de Parques. En 1994, un estudiante de la Universidad de Cincinnati llamado Brendan Murphy, con la ayuda de una beca de la Sociedad para el Diseño Gráfico del Entorno (Society for Environmental Graphic Design, SEGD), realizó algunas excitantes mejoras de los iconos destinados a minusválidos. Más recientemente, el Comité Olímpico de Atlanta seleccionó un equipo de diseño de cinco miembros para desarrollar un programa gráfico completo, así como una nueva serie de pictogramas, para su uso durante los Juegos Olímpicos de verano de 1996.

Cada nuevo conjunto logrado de símbolos pictóricos, no importa cuál sea su grado de utilidad, sólo sirve a un área específica de esfuerzos humanos. ¿Qué tal pues si hubiera una serie universal de pictogramas que cubriera el espectro completo de las actividades públicas? ¿Sería posible diseñar un estudio con el propósito de desarrollar una serie standard universal, internacionalmente reconocida?

En agosto de 1994, la Asociación de Turismo de Portland, Oregón (Portland, Oregon Visitors Association, POVA) se puso en contacto con mi compañía, Design Pacifica International, con el fin de que ayudáramos a mejorar la capacidad de la ciudad de Portland para servir a un número de visitantes extranjeros en rápida expansión. Había resultado dolorosamente obvio que ninguna serie preexistente de pictogramas podía satisfacer por sí sola las necesidades de la metrópolis "global" de hoy. ¿Como podríamos crear símbolos pictóricos standard, internacionalmente reconocidos, para transmitir mensajes sobre todas las áreas de la vida urbana? Tendríamos que hallar pictogramas comunes para transporte, servicios públicos, señales de dirección y salidas, hotel y alojamiento, actividades exteriores y deportivas, reglas y regulaciones, y también para las necesidades de los minusválidos (en conformidad con el ADA). ¿Podría conseguirse tal cosa?

EL PROYECTO PORTLAND

Un standard para la ciudad

En agosto de 1994, el subcomité internacional de la Asociación de Turismo de Portland Oregón (POVA) recomendó que se adoptara un conjunto standard de pictogramas para uso de organizaciones tanto públicas como privadas en el área metropolitana de Portland. El grupo confiaba en que el empleo extendido de pictogramas consistentes y efectivos contribuiría a impulsar la campaña que la ciudad estaba realizando para atraer y mantener su turismo, comercio e inversiones internacionales.

Más tarde ese mismo mes, Dwight Trahin, director de instalaciones del Centro de Comercio Mundial de Portland y miembro del subcomité internacional mencionado, se puso en contacto conmigo. En aquel momento, mi compañía estaba terminando el diseño de un programa de señales exteriores para el mencionado Centro de Comercio Mundial. Casualmente, debido al gran número de visitantes internacionales que frecuentan las instalaciones, habíamos empezado a considerar la necesidad de incluir pictogramas para comunicar mensajes con nuestras señales. Dwight me sugirió que acudiera a una reunión de su subcomité para presentar un breve resumen de nuestro trabajo, así como un repaso de la historia y los usos actuales de los pictogramas.

La presentación tuvo lugar más tarde durante el mismo mes. Puesto que no existía ni un solo conjunto de pictogramas que pudiera comunicar la multitud de mensajes que se requieren para una ciudad entera, los miembros del comité pensaron que habría de crearse un conjunto completo. Según mi opinión, habida cuenta de que ya se empleaban tantos símbolos comunes en todo el mundo, era poco aconsejable diseñar un conjunto nuevo. El comité se mostró de acuerdo y propuso emprender la monumental tarea de compilar conjuntos y símbolos de pictogramas de todo el mundo.

Pronto se hizo bastante claro que necesitábamos un plan de trabajo para abordar el desarrollo de un standard de pictogramas para toda la ciudad. Era preciso crear un proceso. En primer lugar, tendríamos que juntar pictogramas de todo el mundo y categorizarlos por mensaje. Después, tendríamos que evaluarlos y seleccionar los mejores para incluirlos en nuestro nuevo standard. Y, lo más importante, el nuevo standard debería ser adoptado oficialmente por todos los departamentos y agencias de la ciudad, y habría de ser promocionado agresivamente en el sector privado para fomentar su aceptación y uso futuro.

El proceso de evaluación

Durante los seis meses que siguieron, recopilamos varios cientos de pictogramas individuales, y muchos conjuntos de símbolos. Entre los conjuntos preexistentes se incluían el Symbol Signs del D.O.T.; los símbolos para actividades recreativas nacionales, del Cuerpo de Ingenieros del Ejército de Tierra; los símbolos de accesibilidad creados por el SEGD para cumplir con el ADA (Americans with Disabilities Act, o Acta sobre los minusválidos norteamericanos); conjuntos de pictogramas de la Asociación de Hoteles y Moteles Americanos (American Hotel & Motel Association) y la Asociación de Alojamiento de Oregón (Oregon Lodging Association), entre otros. Todos ellos fueron reunidos en un cuaderno para su examen y selección. A continuación, creamos categorías basadas en las necesidades del usuario en un ambiente urbano. El subcomité, encabezado por Andrew Haruyama, director de relaciones internacionales del Ayuntamiento, distribuyó los cuadernos entre sesenta departamentos, agencias y organizaciones de la ciudad. En una serie de reuniones de trabajo, se discutieron nuestros objetivos globales, y se planeó cuidadosamente nuestra manera de proceder.

Decidimos emplear un proceso de evaluación similar al que se usó en el estudio que dio lugar al Symbol Signs, hecho por la AIGA/D.O.T en 1974. Los criterios de evaluación se diseñaron para que los miembros del comité y otros participantes pudieran ponerles una nota o "calificación" a los pictogramas en tres dimensiones distintas aunque interrelacionadas. Se trata de las mismas tres dimensiones que están presentes en toda comunicación visual: semántica, sintáctica y pragmática.

Los pictogramas se representaron individualmente en los cuadernos. Les pedimos a los participantes que marcaran con un círculo sus respuestas en una escala de 1-5 para cada una de las tres dimensiones de diseño, siendo "1" el mínimo grado de efectividad y "5" el mayor. A los participantes se les dieron las siguientes definiciones y preguntas:

La dimensión semántica se refiere a la relación que hay entre una imagen visual y un significado.

-¿Con cuánto éxito representa el mensaje este pictograma?
-¿Entenderá la gente el mensaje que denota este pictograma?
-¿Entenderá la gente de otras culturas este pictograma?
-¿Es fácil de aprender el pictograma?
-¿Ha sido el pictograma muy aceptado previamente?
-¿Contiene el pictograma elementos no relacionados con el mensaje?

La dimensión sintáctica se refiere a la relación que hay entre una imagen visual y otra.

-¿Con qué claridad se relaciona este pictograma, tomado en su conjunto, con los otros pictogramas?

-¿Con qué claridad se relacionan los elementos de este pictograma con los elementos de otros pictogramas?

-¿Es el diseño de este pictograma consistente con el de los demás en su uso de figura/fondo, cuerpo/contorno, superposición, orientación, formato, escala y textura?

-¿Se pueden reconocer los elementos más importantes en primer lugar?

-¿Contradice seriamente este pictograma a los standards o convenciones ya existentes?

La dimensión pragmática se refiere a la relación que se da entre una imagen visual y el usuario.

-¿Puede ver una persona el pictograma?

-¿Puede ser este pictograma seriamente afectado por malas condiciones de luz, ángulos de visión oblicuos, o por cualquier otro "ruido" visual?

-¿Permanece visible este pictograma a lo largo de las distancias típicas de visión?

-¿Es este pictograma especialmente vulnerable al desgaste?

Era importante que el standard definitivo no incluyera un número ni insuficiente ni exagerado de pictogramas. Queríamos adoptar imágenes visuales para los tipos de mensajes de orientación e indicación de direcciones más comúnmente necesitados. Sin embargo, también queríamos evitar una sobrecarga visual, la cual no haría más que disminuir la capacidad del público tanto para ver como para comprender mensajes vitales. A todos los participantes se les pidió, pues, que marcaran cada pictograma/mensaje en sus cuadernos, indicando si debería o no ser incluido en el standard final.

Durante el periodo de dos meses dedicado al examen y evaluación, nos ocupamos también del desarrollo de un programa de software que nos capacitara para procesar los datos y calcular automáticamente los resultados. El programa calculaba una puntuación media y convertía esta información en un porcentaje global para cada una de las tres dimensiones de diseño. Otro porcentaje se formulaba basándose en la indicación del grupo respecto a si el pictograma/mensaje debería incluirse o no en el standard.

Resultados del estudio

Al final del proceso de examen y selección, el subcomité internacional de la POVA se reunió conmigo para repasar los resultados contabilizados. Había una clara disparidad entre los pictogramas que merecían una alta puntuación global por su efectividad y los que se consideraban mediocres. Decidimos considerar para su inclusión en el standard tan sólo aquellos pictogramas que hubieran recibido calificaciones porcentuales por encima de los cincuenta puntos. (Aunque se puede decir que una imagen vale más que mil palabras, ¡nadie quería mil pictogramas para cada mensaje!)

Finalmente, llegó el momento de examinar de cerca cada uno de los pictogramas seleccionados, y considerar los factores que los fortalecerían individualmente y como colección. Se crearon ilustraciones producidas digitalmente para cada pictograma seleccionado. Nuestra preocupación más importante era conseguir un conjunto coherente. Los elementos de los pictogramas -- flechas, figuras humanas, llamas, etc. -- se ilustraron con consistencia y en escalas idénticas. Se decidió que un fondo oscuro con los elementos en blanco daba el nivel óptimo de legibilidad (excepto para aquellos pictogramas que se exhibieran a color). Ya que el objetivo que nos habíamos impuesto era el de evitar el diseño de nuevos pictogramas, nos limitamos a realizar tan solo las alteraciones necesarias.

En las páginas siguientes se muestran ilustraciones del conjunto final de pictogramas seleccionados por los participantes. Las puntuaciones medias colectivas y las clasificaciones porcentuales globales se muestran al lado de cada pictograma.

Ratificación

El 21 de agosto de 1995, la alcaldesa Vera Katz celebró una rueda de prensa en lo alto del World Trade Center Portland. Allí presentó el nuevo Standard Internacional de Pictogramas y desveló el nuevo programa de señalización del World Trade Center Portland -- el primero en incorporar los pictogramas oficiales de la ciudad. "Hoy hemos elevado nuestro rango como ciudad internacional", dijo Katz. "Emprendimos este proyecto porque estábamos de acuerdo en que una imagen vale mil palabras. Estos pictogramas ayudarán a mejorar el ambiente de nuestros negocios internacionales y a hacer nuestra ciudad más "fácil de utilizar" para sus visitantes". El 23 de agosto, la alcaldesa Katz presentó ante el pleno del ayuntamiento una ordenanza en la que se les pedía adoptar formalmente el Standard Internacional de Pictogramas y comenzar la ejecución de la normativa con la sustitución de las señales existentes durante su proceso regular de mantenimiento. La ordenanza fue aprobada con una mayoría aplastante y la ciudad de Portland se convirtió en la primera ciudad de los Estados Unidos que adoptaba formalmente un standard internacional de pictogramas.

¡Habíamos conseguido nuestro objetivo! El Standard Internacional de Pictogramas quedaba establecido. Una nueva conciencia se había despertado y se habían iniciado los pasos para afianzar una metrópolis más "fácil para el usuario". Los esfuerzos para promover y fomentar el uso del nuevo standard continúan en Portland. De mayor significación "global" son los planes, a punto ahora de ultimarse, para pedirles a las ciudades hermanadas con Portland (actualmente unas nueve) su apoyo y adopción del standard.

Portland tiene motivos más que suficientes para sentirse orgullosa de este logro. El hecho de que departamentos municipales, agencias y organizaciones privadas se reúnan, unifiquen sus criterios y -- en el plazo relativamente corto de un año -- produzcan algo de valor mundial, no puede por menos que calificarse de milagro moderno. Portland ha mandado señales de bienvenida a sus vecinos globales. El tiempo dirá si éstos deciden responder con esas mismas señales.

Participantes en el proceso de evaluación y selección

El subcomité internacional de la POVA y los distintos departamentos, agencias y organizaciones de la ciudad de Portland no cejaron en su propósito de conseguir el objetivo de crear un standard Internacional de Pictogramas. Personalmente, quiero quitarme el sombrero ante todos aquellos que participaron en este estudio, y reconocer su esfuerzo infatigable, así como la enorme cantidad de tiempo que todos dedicaron.

LA CREACIÓN DE UN STANDARD MUNDIAL

Un "standard vivo"

Llegamos ahora a nuestro desafío más importante: crear un estudio dinámico y mundial de los Pictogramas Internacionales. Queremos mantener el Standard tan flexible como nos sea posible. Para mantener su utilidad a largo plazo, debe convertirse en un "standard vivo", que cambie según cambian las necesidades del usuario.

Para responder al desafío, Design Pacifica International ha emprendido una campaña de multimedia para estimular una conciencia, distribución y participación internacionales. Este libro, con primeras ediciones en inglés y español, constituye un elemento clave de esa campaña. Ya se han hecho planes para futuras ediciones en otras lenguas.

Para llegar a tanta gente como sea posible en todo el mundo, también hemos creado un CD ROM interactivo (de plataforma mixta, Macintosh y Windows). Este permite a los usuarios leer PictoFacts‰ (Historia de los pictogramas e instrucciones de uso); acceder a PictoView (para ver los pictogramas por categoría, etc.); leer acerca del Proyecto Portland y ponerse al tanto de las cuestiones relacionadas con el cumplimiento de las reglas ADA para señalización. El CD también contiene ilustraciones de los pictogramas preparadas digitalmente, junto a PictoFont (un tipo de letra TrueType para pictogramas, creado por Design Pacifica International).

Para fomentar la participación mundial, tanto el libro como el paquete de CD ROM incluyen hojas de calificación/evaluación. Todos los que rellenen y devuelvan la hoja de calificación recibirán a cambio un regalo gratis.

La World Wide Web:
http://www.pictograms.com

Los visitantes globales pueden acceder a nuestra hoja en la Internet para evaluar la efectividad de los pictogramas exhibidos. Como queremos continuar la búsqueda de nuevos pictogramas/mensajes para mantener nuestro Standard fácil de usar, periódicamente anunciaremos candidatos que estén en proceso de evaluación. Los resultados serán automáticamente enviados por correo electrónico a nuestras oficinas. Estos resultados, a su vez, se compilarán en nuevas bases de datos para actualizar cada 30 meses el standard, en forma de libros y CD ROMs adicionales.

Ud. puede participar

Nuestra oferta de una participación continua y global hace del Standard Internacional de Pictogramas algo único. Muchos conjuntos de símbolos se han desarrollado y estudiado por diversos comités y organizaciones de todo el mundo. Otros han sido diseñados por individuos que disfrutaban de becas temporales. Este es el primero que trata de ser a la vez continuo y abierto a la colaboración mundial.

La siguiente página es su hoja personal de evaluación. Por favor, siga cuidadosamente las instrucciones, arranque el formulario después de rellenarlo y envíenoslo por correo. Nuestra base de datos computarizada procesará las respuestas. Esta es su oportunidad de participar en un fórum internacional. Esperamos con interés su respuesta.

CÓMO USAR LOS PICTOGRAMAS

Recomendaciones para su empleo

Los pictogramas son sólo efectivos si son familiares, y se hacen familiares sólo cuando se emplean consistente y universalmente. Considérese la señal de Stop. Virtualmente todo el mundo en el planeta la reconoce. Porque está en todas partes; y en todas las partes donde aparece, tiene prácticamente el mismo aspecto. Si el Standard Internacional de Pictogramas se va a convertir en universalmente efectivo, deberá emplearse consistentemente en todo el mundo. Ese es el objetivo. Para alcanzarlo, ofrecemos las siguientes recomendaciones. Tienen la finalidad de asegurar la legibilidad, fomentar el reconocimiento público y permitir flexibilidad respecto a condiciones del entorno y problemas de diseño específicos.

Fondo y figura: Aunque es aceptable usar un fondo claro y una figura oscura, se aconseja mostrar los pictogramas con fondo oscuro y figura clara. Por un fenómeno óptico conocido como el efecto ona, una figura clara tiende a "sangrar visualmente" o extenderse contra un fondo oscuro, pareciendo más grande que en el caso inverso. Un fondo claro, por otra parte, tiene a "comerse" visualmente la figura, haciéndola parecer más pequeña. Esto se cumple con todos los pictogramas, pero especialmente con las señales de letras.

Fondo y figura deberían mantenerse intactos siempre que sea posible. Con las señales, sin embargo, es aceptable usar sólo la figura, ya que el trasfondo de la señal sirve como fondo. Cuando varios pictogramas se usan en una sola señal, fondo y figura deberían mantenerse siempre intactos para poder distinguir cada mensaje.

Color: Los fondos oscuros se deberían limitar al negro, colores oscuros neutros (grises y marrones), verde bosque, azul marino, etc. No se recomiendan los colores llamativos, ya que tonalidades como el rojo, azul o amarillo intensos están diseñadas exclusivamente para pictogramas de la categoría reguladora.

Tamaño: Aparte de los requerimientos del ADA, que se discutirán más tarde en este mismo capítulo, el tamaño de un pictograma depende de su uso y situación. Si un pictograma se usa como señal o sobre una señal, se aconseja determinar el tamaño en el ambiente en que se va a

instalar. Un pictograma de 12 pulgadas (30 cm) de altura (fondo y figura) puede percibirse óptimamente desde aproximadamente 100 pies (30 m), y un pictograma de 6 pulgadas (15 cm) se puede reconocer desde aproximadamente 50 pies (15 m). (Estas pautas se basan en el Standard Internacional de Pictogramas y en la complejidad media de las figuras de la colección. Los pictogramas con figuras menos intrincadas se podrán leer desde mayores distancias.)

Presentación de los pictogramas sobre las señales: Una señal que muestra un pictograma es, en la mayor parte de los casos, suficiente para transmitir un mensaje. Sin embargo, se recomienda que los pictogramas vayan acompañados de mensajes y/o señales con caracteres. Bajo ninguna circunstancia se deberían añadir caracteres al fondo del pictograma. Se aconseja que los mensajes/leyendas se coloquen directamente bajo el pictograma o a su lado.

Cuestiones de conformidad con la señalización para minusválidos (ADA)

El Acta sobre los minusválidos norteamericanos (Americans with Disabilities Act), elevada a categoría de ley en 1990, está diseñada para conceder a todos los minusválidos norteamericanos oportunidades y acceso iguales a los del resto de la población. Como con toda legislación, muchos detalles se dejan a la interpretación de ello. Las regulaciones establecidas con respecto a la señalización caen dentro de éstas. La información aquí provista es tan sólo una interpretación, y no debería confundirse con consejos o recomendaciones legales. El autor y la editorial no asumen responsabilidad legal, ni expresa ni implícita, por cualquier error u omisión que se cometan en este texto.

Identificación de instalaciones y prestaciones accesibles: entradas, aseos sanitarios e instalaciones de baño.
El pictograma internacional de accesibilidad se debe exhibir en entradas accesibles si no todas las entradas lo son. Las direcciones, incluyendo el pictograma, se deben exhibir desde las entradas inaccesibles a las accesibles. Directrices semejantes han de aplicarse a los aseos sanitarios e instalaciones de baño.

Areas de auxilio y salvamento
Las áreas de auxilio y salvamento deben identificarse con señales iluminadas y/o no iluminadas, incluyendo el pictograma internacional de accesibilidad. Debe haber presentes instrucciones para usar el área durante emergencias. Las salidas inaccesibles deben ser identificadas como tales. En aquellos lugares donde no todas las salidas sean accesibles, las señales, incluyendo el pictograma, deben dirigir a los visitantes a las áreas de auxilio y salvamento.

Teléfonos públicos
Los teléfonos con texto han de identificarse con un pictograma TDD. Los teléfonos con control de volumen se deben identificar con el pictograma de control de volumen telefónico. Allá donde no todas las instalaciones telefónicas estén equipadas, se han de exhibir direcciones, incluyendo el pictograma apropiado, que dirijan desde los teléfonos no equipados a los equipados.

Sistemas de escucha asistida
Los sistemas de escucha asistida se han de identificar con el pictograma internacional de pérdida del oído, junto con una descripción del sistema provisto.

Señales de designación de alojamiento permanente
El uso de pictogramas sobre señales de designación de alojamiento permanente es opcional, pero allá donde se usen, deben colocarse sobre un fondo o borde de como mínimo 6 pulgadas (15 cm) de altura. Una descripción equivalente, escrita táctilmente en Braille Grado 2 (con un relieve mínimo de 1/32 de pulgada (0.7 mm) sobre la superficie de la señal, con letras exclusivamente mayúsculas de entre 5/8 y 2 pulgadas (1,5-5 cm) de altura del molde) se debe colocar directamente debajo del pictograma (con la excepción de las flechas) y no puede introducirse en el fondo de 6 pulgadas (15 cm) del pictograma.

La legislación y directrices del ADA (ADAAG) se pueden obtener a través del Departamento de Justicia de los Estados Unidos, llamando al

(202) 514-0301 (voz)
(202) 514-0383 (TDD)

La Sociedad de diseño gráfico medioambiental (SEGD) ha publicado un *Libro Blanco* en el que se proveen clarificaciones e interpretaciones de la regulación concerniente a los requisitos de señalización ADA. Este documento se puede obtener a través del SEGD llamando al:

(voz) (202) 638-5555, o escribiendo a la siguiente dirección electrónica: SEGDoffice@aol.com

Sobre el autor

Todd Pierce es presidente de Design Pacifica International, una compañía especializada en diseño gráfico a juego con el entorno con oficinas en San Francisco y en Portland, Oregón. Dicha compañía ha llevado a cabo proyectos de señalización para el World Trade Center (Centro de Comercio Mundial) de Portland, el Museo de Ciencia e Industria de Oregón, la Oregon Health Sciences University, el Lewis & Clark College y Powell's City of Books, la librería de libros nuevos y usados más grande del mundo. Entre otros proyectos importantes, cabe mencionar también un plan maestro de información y señalización para la ciudad de Newport, Oregón, y el Standard Internacional de Pictogramas, una compilación y estandarización de pictogramas procedentes de todo el mundo.

Pierce inició su carrera profesional en 1981, como director de diseño gráfico para las oficinas neoyorquinas de Perkins & Will Architects. En 1983, a los 22 años de edad, fundó su propia compañía de diseño gráfico y comunicaciones de márketing. Entre los trabajos más importantes de esta empresa, se incluyen un nuevo plan de señalización para el sistema suburbano de Nueva York y gráficos a juego con el entorno para la Swiss Bank Tower, la sede mundial de Deloitte + Touche, y el hotel y complejo comercial Carlton Centre de Johannesburgo, Sudáfrica; asimismo, la compañía ha realizado proyectos de señalización para muchas de las corporaciones, hospitales y bufetes de abogados más importantes del mundo.

A lo largo de los últimos diez años, su trabajo ha merecido numerosos galardones, y ha sido presentado frecuentemente en publicaciones de diseño, tanto nacionales como internacionales. Pierce ha enseñado diseño gráfico a juego con el entorno en la Parsons School of Design de Nueva York y en el Lewis & Clark College de Portland.

Appendix

Selected Bibliography

Henry Dreyfuss
Symbol Sourcebook
1972
McGraw-Hill Book Publishers
330 West 42nd Street
New York, NY 10036

The American Institute of Graphic Arts for the U.S. Department of Transportation
Symbol Signs
2nd Edition, 1993
The American Institute of Graphic Arts
1059 Third Avenue
New York, NY 10021

Nigel Holmes
Designing Pictorial Symbols
1985
Watson-Guptill Publications
1515 Broadway
New York, NY 10036

Philip B. Meggs
A History of Graphic Design
2nd Edition, 1992
Van Nostrand Reinhold
115 Fifth Avenue
New York, NY 10003

SEGD
The Americans with Disabilities Act
White Paper
2nd Edition, 1993
The Society for Environmental Graphic Design
401 F Street, NW
Washington, DC 20001

218